The

AUTOBIOGRAPHY

of

SANTA CLAUS

JEREMY P. TARCHER/PENGUIN

a member of Penguin Group (USA) Inc.

New York

The

AUTOBIOGRAPHY

of

SANTA CLAUS

as told to JEFF GUINN

Most Tarcher/Penguin books are available at special quantity discounts for bulk purchase for sales promotions, premiums, fund-raising, and educational needs. Special books or book excerpts also can be created to fit specific needs. For details, write Penguin Group (USA) Inc. Special Markets, 375 Hudson Street, New York, NY 10014.

The recipe contained in this book is to be followed exactly as written. The publisher is not responsible for your specific health or allergy needs that may require medical supervision. The publisher is not responsible for any adverse reactions to the recipe contained in this book.

Jeremy P. Tarcher/Penguin
a member of
Penguin Group (USA) Inc.
375 Hudson Street
New York, NY 10014
www.penguin.com

First published in 1994 by The Summit Group
First Jeremy P. Tarcher/Penguin Edition 2003
Copyright © 1994 by Jeff Guinn
Illustrations by Dorit Rabinovitch

Library of Congress Cataloging-in-Publication Data
Guinn, Jeff.
The autobiography of Santa Claus / as told to Jeff Guinn.
p.   cm.
Includes bibliographical references (p.   ).
ISBN 1-58542-265-7
1. Santa Claus—Fiction.   I. Title.
PS3557.U375A97   2003   2003053722
813'.54—dc21

Printed in the United States of America
5   7   9   10   8   6   4

This book is printed on acid-free paper. ∞

Book design by Amanda Dewey

Contents

Editor's Preface

I WROTE A BOOK WITH SANTA CLAUS. Not too many people can say that. In fact, I'm the only one I know of.

In just a page or two, Santa will begin telling you about his life, and in his words, not mine. But I thought you might want to know how this book came to be written in the first place. It was sort of an accident, but a wonderful one.

A few Decembers ago, my newspaper printed a story I'd written about little-known facts of Christmas—why it's celebrated on that specific date, how the name "Saint Nicholas" was changed to "Santa Claus" in America, and some other things. Most of us take our Christmas traditions for granted. We have no idea about when some of our favorite customs started, or who was responsible. I enjoyed writing the story, but I pretty much forgot about it right after it appeared in print.

A few months later, the receptionist in the newspaper's lobby called my third-floor office and said a man was asking to see me. "He seems very friendly," she explained. "He says his name is Felix."

The fellow was about average height and had an engaging smile. He was dressed in an ordinary gray business suit, wore glasses, and was a bit overweight. I guessed he was in his early forties.

"You're Felix . . . ?" I asked, expecting him to tell me his last name.

"Just Felix." He grinned as he removed a bit of folded newspaper from his coat pocket. It was a copy of my Christmas story.

"We read this with a lot of interest," Felix said. "It's all right as far as it goes, but it didn't really have much important information. So we took it to him, and he said he believed it was time to tell the real story, all of it."

Not pleased to hear my story criticized, I replied sharply, "Who exactly is 'we,' and who exactly is 'him'?"

Felix's smile grew even wider. "I can't tell you yet. What we hope you'll do is agree to accompany me on a trip. When we get to where we're going, you'll get your answers. Please—don't worry. This isn't a trick. It's just that we're people who value our privacy. You're going to be asked to help with a writing project, but before we leave, you must agree not to tell anyone about who you met, or where—that's if you decide you don't want to get involved."

Like most writers, I'm curious by nature. Besides, there was something about Felix that made me trust him. I agreed to his conditions. We left the next day to meet this mysterious "him."

I can't describe the trip itself. Obviously, we went to see Santa Claus at the North Pole, but part of my agreement with Santa is that I can't reveal how we got there.

When we arrived, you can imagine my shock at being greeted by an instantly familiar figure. In person, Santa is everything you'd want him to be—wise and jolly, white-bearded and thick-bellied, and, above all, genuinely warm and caring.

Before we had our private talk, Santa introduced me to some of his helpers—his "friends," he insisted on calling them. My amazement at actually meeting Santa Claus doubled when I found myself shaking hands with some of the most famous people who ever lived and, apparently, hadn't died. I won't name them here—Santa will do that in his own time.

Once we were finally in Santa's study, seated in front of a warm fire and munching chocolate chip cookies, he explained why he had invited me to the North Pole.

"The true story of Christmas, and my part in it, is as wonderful and complicated as the world itself," Santa said. "Very few people really know much about the holiday at all. For some time, Layla has been urging me to tell the real story, so everyone will understand Christmas and Santa Claus better."

"And Layla is . . . ?" I asked.

"My wife, of course," Santa chuckled. "She's a much more interesting person than the meek little lady people usually picture when they think of Mrs. Santa Claus. Anyway, I'm not a writer myself, so I thought I might find one who'd record my story as I tell it, then turn it into a book for everyone to read. The story you wrote for your newspaper convinces me that you truly love Christmas, although I'm afraid you don't know nearly as much about it as you think you do."

How could I refuse? I called home, told my family I'd be away for a while, and began helping Santa with his book. It seemed more like fun than work. Santa's stories were full of adventure and wonder. Sometimes, Layla, Felix, or other friends would join us and add their comments.

Throughout the project, Santa insisted that our book be historically accurate. "We want readers to learn some things about world history as well as the history of Christmas," he constantly repeated. Whenever any date or other fact was in doubt, we consulted history books. So, as amazing as it might seem, just about everyone whose name you read here really did exist. Only a few of the main characters—Phillip, Felix, Layla, Dorothea, and Willie Skokan—can't be found in history books, because they valued their privacy so much.

Well, that's enough from me. Santa's the one whose voice you want and need to hear, so prepare yourself for a unique story that's equal parts history and magic.

In closing, let me assure you doubters—there really is a Santa Claus. I learned from working on this book that you don't need to go to the North Pole to find him. It's only necessary to look into your own heart.

Jeff Guinn
Fort Worth, Texas

Foreword

You're right to believe in me.

Oh, I know it's hard sometimes. There always are people eager to tell you there isn't a Santa Claus, that I'm just a story made up long ago and trotted out every Christmas since. I suppose I should be angry with them, but I feel sorry for them instead. Have you ever noticed that it's always unhappy people who attack the things happy people believe in? That's been my observation, at least, and I suppose I've been around long enough to know.

So let's start with this. I've decided it's time to tell the real story of Santa Claus, and to have it told by the one who knows it best—me. It's a long story, going back the better part of two thousand years. I'll try not to bore you too much with dates and places, but there are important times and people in my life you should know more about—my wife, for one, and Felix, who was my first helper fifteen centuries ago, and others. Without many faithful friends, my role in Christmas wouldn't have been possible, and that's one reason I want to tell my tale. I always get the credit. From the beginning, my philosophy has been, "It's better to give than to receive," and I want to see the credit properly shared among all those who deserve it.

I remember one time, for instance, when the pilgrims maintained it wasn't right to celebrate Christmas at all. They decided anyone caught observing the holiday would be punished, and I found myself telling Felix that I should just give up ever doing my holiday rounds in the new land called America. Felix convinced me otherwise, of course; we'll tell that story in its proper time. But it's a good example of why someone else deserves some of the glory. Probably I was just feeling discouraged when I made that remark to Felix—even Santa Claus gets discouraged sometimes—and almost certainly I would simply have waited the pilgrims out. Still, it's also possible that without Felix's encouraging words, no child in the United States would ever have awakened Christmas morning to find filled stockings and a present from old Santa under the tree.

Another reason I'm writing this book is to clear up some matters that apparently have troubled too many people for too long. On Christmas Eve, for instance, they wonder how Santa can possibly get around to the house of every deserving child in the whole wide world. Why do I have different names in different countries if I'm just one person? Do my helpers and I really live at the North Pole, and do reindeer really know how to fly?

I'll tell what I can, but I must say this right away: There are some answers I don't know, either. This is the difference, the very important difference, between illusion and magic. Illusion is when something happens that seems impossible, but eventually can be figured out. Magic is when something happens that can't be understood.

Quite simply, illusion is explained, but magic just *is*. There's some illusion in what I do, but there's a fair share of magic, too. You'll learn about times I couldn't quite understand what was happening to me, and how I finally realized there are some things that can't be understood, just accepted.

But what I hope you'll learn above all else is that the real magic of Christmas involves love, and that the greatest joy is giving rather than getting. Just as this isn't a perfect world, Christmas isn't a perfect holiday, and won't be until all human beings on this beautiful planet can live together in harmony. No single person can make this happen, but if we each do what we can, then there's still hope that one Christmas Day we'll find ourselves enjoying the most wonderful gift possible—complete peace on Earth, and goodwill from everyone to everyone.

Well! That was quite a speech I let myself make! Layla—I suppose she's better known as Mrs. Claus—would point out I was sounding like quite an old windbag! "Get on with the story!" she'd say if she were reading this. And she'd be right; it's time to begin. After all, I don't want to put you to sleep.

Unless, of course, it's Christmas Eve.

Dizzy from the knock on the head and smelly from pig droppings, I staggered to my feet, grabbed my ladder, and hurried back toward the inn. Shem was making a fearful uproar inside his house, screaming to his daughters to wake up and help him catch the thief.

ONE

My Earliest Memories

live at the snowy North Pole now, but my life began surrounded by sand. I was born in a country that was then called *Lycia;* it's since been absorbed into the nation of Turkey, which I suppose is appropriate, considering what many families like to eat for their Christmas dinner. Lycia was located along the southwestern border of the land across the Mediterranean Sea from Egypt and Israel.

The year of my birth is recorded as 280 A.D., or two hundred and eighty years after what is now considered the "official" birth year of a much more important baby, whose name was Jesus. Actually, records weren't kept as carefully in those days, so no one is really sure in which year Jesus was born. The main thing is, I was born about three centuries later in the Lycian town of Patara. Sometimes I find it odd, and other times amusing, that I know the exact details of when I came into this world, but have no idea how long I'm going to stay. Patara was a prosperous village as villages went in those days, meaning many of the four hundred people living there got enough to eat and had houses to live in. Today my hometown would seem very primitive—no indoor bathrooms, no video games, no cars roaring up and down its streets. But everybody knew everybody else's name.

My father's name was Epiphaneos and my mother was called Nonna. They were quite old when I was born, probably in their fifties. People didn't live as long then as they do now—maybe to sixty if they were lucky. We didn't have much in the way of medicine, and everybody ate what they wanted without worrying about calories. Anyway, I arrived long after my parents had given up hope of having a baby. I was quite a surprise to them! They celebrated by naming me Nicholas, which means "victorious." It was a name I liked very much. No one used nicknames in those days, so I was always Nicholas and never Nick or Nicky. I acquired my nicknames much later in life.

We were a Christian family. As I grew up and learned more and more about my religion, one thing Jesus said always stayed with me: that we should treat other people the way we would want them to treat us. That made sense to me even as a little boy. Other parts of being a Christian weren't as much fun. There were days you were supposed to fast, and I always liked to eat. Even goat cheese tasted good to me. One of the sadder things about living now at the North Pole is that I just can't get goat cheese anymore. Maybe a few of you reading this book will leave me some next Christmas Eve instead of the usual cookies, though I'm certainly glad to have the cookies—especially homemade chocolate chip, if anyone's taking notes.

I was given a good education, by which I mean I was taught to read and write Hebrew, Greek, and Latin. There were a lot of languages, because we lived in what was called a "melting pot," or a place through which people of all different countries and races might pass. If by chance someone came to our family inn and spoke only Hebrew, he might go on to the next town and the next inn if we weren't able to answer back in Hebrew.

Being able to read and write in several languages made me something of a scholar. There wasn't any formal schooling then. Boys learned as much as their parents wanted them to. Girls, I'm sorry to say, were seldom allowed to go to school at all. People thought they were only suited to stay home, keep house, and someday raise children of their own. I'm glad people finally learned better, although it took much too long. (I hope my wife, Layla, will be pleased I mentioned this so early in my book; it was always an important point to her, as you'll learn when I get to the part of my story about when I met her. But that's a hundred years after the time we're talking about now.)

My parents guessed they wouldn't live long enough to see me grow up, and they were right. They died peacefully during the year I was nine—my father first and my mother a few months later. I loved them very much and grieved over their loss. I believed in heaven and felt they'd gone to live with Jesus, but I wished they could have gone on living with me. All these centuries later I remember them very well. As long as people are remembered by someone, they're never completely gone. My parents were generous people, and I'm sure that somewhere they've enjoyed watching their son go on to such an unexpected—and long—career.

It was arranged that I would be put in the care of guardians, the priests of the local church. There were five of them, all very busy most days traveling from our village to other smaller towns. These trips could be long ones. Often, there could be forty miles or more of desert between one place and the next. By choice these priests were poor, giving up nice clothes and good food for the privilege of serving others. They didn't even have oxcarts or donkeys to take them where they wanted to go. They walked. I admired them, but I didn't think much of all that walking.

I stayed at the inn where I'd lived with my parents. The priests had papers from my father allowing them to spend the money I inherited as they saw fit. Therefore, they paid the staff of the inn a little extra to make sure I received all my meals and got my clothes washed when they were sufficiently dirty, which usually meant once every few weeks. Lots of sand blew through the air and there were no washing machines. Clothes were washed in big pots of boiling water, and it was a chore to haul buckets of water from the river back to the inn. I didn't mind my clothes staying dirty awhile, since I was always the one told to go fill the buckets.

My life stayed the same for several more years, but as I grew older I noticed that some people in Patara weren't as well-off as I was. It didn't seem right that I ate two or three good meals every day when some of the poorer families were lucky to have a little bread, and perhaps even went hungry once in a while. I found I couldn't enjoy my nice clothes when neighbors had to wear rags. I talked about it with the priests, and they all agreed I was right to feel uncomfortable. But they said I would have to decide for myself how to deal with those feelings.

There was one priest in particular named Phillip. His job was to take care of the church's goats and chickens. He looked rather like a goat himself, right down to his scraggly little white chin-beard. I helped Phillip with the animals sometimes, and he was someone whose opinion I especially respected.

Lycia and the Mediterranean Sea

"How can I stop feeling guilty about having so many things when my neighbors have nothing?" I asked him one day. We'd just fed the goats and were standing alongside their smelly stall.

"The answer is already in your heart, Nicholas," he replied, tugging at his beard. "You've heard the words of Jesus. The richest men in heaven will be the ones who gave away the most during their time on Earth."

I knew he meant I should give away most of my things, such as my warm clothes to those wearing rags, my good food to those who were hungry, and so forth. I was willing to do it, but even simple generosity had its problems, the most important of which was other people's pride. Adults would feel ashamed if it became known they'd accepted charity from a twelve-year-old boy. I said good-bye to Phillip and went back to the inn to think about it some more.

That night I was sitting in the inn's dining hall, still feeling troubled. I'd had my usual nice supper of bread and cheese and fat juicy olives, washing it all down with lots of fresh goat's milk. By this time, most of the guests had been fed and were back in their rooms. A few men from my village were sitting in front of the fireplace talking about Shem, another citizen of Patara who'd once been rich, only to fall on hard times. He'd made some money selling camels and then invested the money in two freight ships. Sometime later, the ships were caught in a storm and sank. Shem's fortune sank with them. Now he went from house to house in Patara asking to mend fishing nets for whatever anyone wanted to pay him. His wife had died years earlier, and he was trying to raise three daughters all by himself. And that was really Shem's problem, these men were saying.

"All three girls of marriage age, and no money for even one dowry," one of the men remarked. "It's sadder still because each has a young man who wants to marry her. I think the oldest daughter's fifteen, too."

One of the other men made a clucking noise with his tongue. "Fifteen! Another few years and it'll be much too late for her to ever marry. Oh, well, it makes no difference. Shem will never be able to put aside money for their dowries in a hundred years."

I should explain here that back then people got married at much younger ages. Girls as young as twelve or thirteen were considered ready to be brides. Boys could wait a little longer, maybe until they were fifteen or sixteen. Shem's daughters were fifteen, thirteen, and twelve, meaning all three were old enough to be married.

But the dowry custom complicated things. When a man married a woman, he had to support her for the rest of her life, so the bride's father was expected to give his daughter's new husband some money to help pay these future expenses. I thought the idea was silly when I first heard it, and still do. It was just another way in those unenlightened days that women were treated as though they weren't as good as men.

So these poor girls all had suitors who wanted to marry them, but custom wouldn't allow those marriages to take place as long as Shem didn't have money for dowries. Then I had a wonderful idea. I had money, even if Shem didn't. I could give him enough money for each girl to have a fine dowry and be able to marry her suitor. That would make the daughters happy. Since Shem wouldn't have to support them anymore, it might mean he wouldn't have to work as hard mending nets. Then everyone would be pleased, most of all me, because I would have done something generous and shared my wealth.

I went back up to my room and pulled out the small sack of silver coins I kept under my bedding. If necessary, I could have gone to any one of several people in town who were keeping some of the money my parents had left for me, but when I spilled the coins out on my bed I saw I really had plenty for the dowries—twelve coins in all. Four silver coins per daughter would be just right.

But how could I give the girls the money without shaming their father? If I walked up to Shem's door and told him what I was doing, he would surely feel humiliated. And if I just left the sack of coins on his doorstep, some passerby might steal it.

The next day I went back to talk a little more to Phillip, the priest. This time he was gathering eggs and asked me to help him. We went from hen to hen, chatting all the while. As we walked, I performed some handstands, and then balanced myself on the log fence surrounding the chicken coops. As a boy, I wasn't as heavy as I am now.

"I see you're athletic besides being so clever, Nicholas," Phillip said. "You say you don't want to embarrass Shem. Well, do you think you can climb a ladder? His house has lots of windows, and everyone opens all their shutters at night so cool breezes can blow through them."

Phillip never actually told me I should sneak into Shem's house and leave the money, but his meaning was clear. It sounded like an adventure, and I set out to give my secret gifts that very night.

I waited until well after dark, when everyone in the village was asleep. We all got up very early, often before dawn, so we never stayed up too late at night.

Phillip

I wore my darkest robes and carried a small ladder borrowed from the workers' shed down the street, and moments after leaving the inn I was standing outside Shem's house.

Although he was poor, Shem and his daughters still lived in the house he had built when he was rich. It was just one story tall, but the walls were higher than those of most houses, rising almost twice as high as my head. The windows were up high, too, closer to the roof than to the floor. This was because heat and light were provided by fires, and as the smoke rose toward the ceiling it was supposed to waft out the open windows. Often, though, the winds blew in off the desert and the smoke just came back into the houses, making people's eyes water. Chimneys weren't invented yet.

I listened outside the house for a few moments. No one inside was making a sound. I guessed the house would have three rooms, one a big family room where meals were prepared and eaten, a bedroom for the three girls, and a bedroom for their father. I intended to leave the silver coins in Shem's room, but as I stood outside his house I began to wonder whether—when he woke in the morning and found the coins—he'd know they were for his daughters' dowries. A better plan would be to leave the coins in the room where the daughters slept. If they really had suitors who wanted to marry them, they'd know how the money should be spent.

My next problem was finding out which room belonged to the girls. The only way to find out was to look. I leaned my ladder against a wall close to the nearest window and climbed up. The shutters were half open. I peeked inside. It was very dark in there. There wasn't any fire lit, at least in that room, although I could hear the sound of someone snoring. Was it Shem or one of his daughters? I poked my head farther inside the room. Just then the desert wind gusted and the heavy wooden shutter was blown hard against my head. There was a loud thud as shutter and skull came together. I yelped with pain, waking up the snorer, who turned out to be Shem

"Who's there?" he barked. "If you're a thief, I have a stick!"

I had no desire to meet Shem's stick. My head hurt enough already. Forgetting I was on a ladder, I pulled back from the window, toppled over into the street, and landed on a pile of straw. Pigs had spent time in that straw, and had deposited fragrant souvenirs. Dizzy from the knock on the head and smelly from pig droppings, I staggered to my feet, grabbed my ladder, and hurried back toward the inn. Shem was making a fearful uproar inside his house, screaming to his daughters to wake up and help him catch the thief. Startled, they began screaming, too.

As I ran, I heard behind me the sound of doors being thrown open and the voices of Shem's neighbors calling to ask him what had happened. Luckily, I was able to put the ladder away, creep back to my room, and slip into my night robes without anyone seeing me. I lay awake until almost dawn, my head throbbing and my nose offended by the way I smelled.

As soon as I could, without attracting notice, I went out into the early morning to fetch a bucket of water so I could wash off most of the odor. Over breakfast at the inn I heard people talking about how brave Shem had been to fight off six thieves who'd tried to break into his home. It put me in a poor mood.

When I'd finished eating, I went back to talk to Phillip. I didn't have to tell him what had happened. With no television or other way to hear world news, local tales were our main entertainment. Gossip spread fast.

"I hear a dozen burglars tried to break into old Shem's house last night," Phillip laughed. "He had a stick handy, I'm told, and beat some of them badly, although none so severely that they couldn't run away afterward. Did the noise wake you, by any chance?"

"I hit my head on a shutter and fell off the ladder into a pile of pig-fouled hay," I replied sourly. "I think this marks the end of my gift-giving."

To my surprise, Phillip's face reddened with anger. He started to say something, caught himself, turned redder, and finally said quietly, "You've suffered enough, have you? The pain of a fall into some dirty hay was so awful, you've forgotten the pain of Shem and his daughters? These feelings you've described to me, your pity for those with less than you and how you'd like to do good things for others, were lost at the same time you lost your balance on that ladder?"

"Not really," I protested. "I still feel sad for Shem's family, and for anyone else in need. It's just that I'm apparently not very good at giving presents. Look what a mess I made of it last night."

Phillip looked at me for a long moment, then said thoughtfully, "Do you recall the story of the three kings who traveled far to give gifts to the baby Jesus?"

I did; it was a favorite tale of mine. Apparently, three royal persons—or magicians, or astronomers, depending on who told the story—saw a bright star in the sky and knew they should follow it to where a special baby would be. They brought presents for this unknown infant—precious things such as gold and spices. They had to go a long way, riding camels for the most part. Eventually, they found Jesus, presented their gifts, and then went back to wherever it was that they came from.

"Of course I remember the three kings," I said to Phillip. "Why do you ask?"

"Did the kings have an easy time finding the Christ-child?" he replied. "Did they give up when they weren't successful in giving him their gifts on the first night of their journey?"

"Shem's daughters aren't the baby Jesus," I said sulkily.

"And you're not a king, either," Phillip responded, his words trapping me neatly.

"Your point is made," I conceded. "I'll try again tonight."

Actually, it was four nights before I could try again. It took that long before Shem and some of the other men of the village stopped lying in wait in the night shadows, watching to see if the band of thieves would again try to rob Shem's house, or perhaps another house in Patara. Every time I sneaked out of the inn, I quickly caught glimpses of people hiding behind donkey stalls and low fences. And each night I went back to my bed thinking, "That's enough. I won't try again tomorrow night." But I did, and finally on the fourth night no one was lying in wait for the thieves' return.

I got my ladder and quietly walked to Shem's house. I leaned the ladder by another high window and climbed up. I peeked through the open shutter and knew instantly that I had picked the right room this time. There was a low fire burning in the grate, and in its dim light I could see the shadows of three figures sleeping on rumpled bedding.

A new problem presented itself. It was a short drop down to the floor, perhaps six feet. I could do it easily, but once inside, how would I get back out again? The door to the street would undoubtedly be latched, and, anyway, it was in old Shem's room. I had no intention of waking him up and giving him a real chance to beat a presumed burglar with his stick.

The only thing to do was balance on the windowsill, draw up the ladder and place it inside the room. Then I could climb down, leave the coins, climb to the windowsill, pull up the ladder, lean it back out into the street, and climb down.

The first part of this plan worked admirably. My ladder was made of lashed-together wood, and I made little noise pulling it up from the street, easing it over the windowsill and then down into the girls' room. As soon as it touched the floor, I swung myself about and climbed down inside the house.

But just as I stepped away from the ladder, one of the sleeping girls began to moan from a bad dream. It was Sara, Shem's youngest daughter. As Sara whimpered, both her older sisters, Celina and Ruth, began to toss about, too. I worried either might awaken, get up to comfort Sara, and see me standing there. I froze where I stood, scarcely daring to breathe. After a few moments Sara seemed to settle back into a deeper sleep. I counted to fifty, then cautiously reached inside my robe for the pouch of coins. It was my intention to leave four coins under each girl's pillow; after all, my parents had often left little presents under my pillow when I was asleep.

I tiptoed toward Sara and was just reaching toward her pillow with four coins in my hand, when she again began to twitch and whimper. I jumped back and tripped over my own feet. I fought to recover my balance and nearly fell into the fire. Fortunately, I missed the flames and instead fell on the hard dirt floor. There was a soft thump as my head bounced off the floor. I expected the thump to wake the girls and their father, too, and briefly thought my head hadn't yet received all the punishment it was going to get. Fortunately for me, Shem didn't come rushing from his room. None of the girls woke up, either.

Still, it had been too close a call. I wanted to leave the coins behind and make my escape.

I was afraid to come near the girls again. My luck couldn't hold up much longer. Looking around the room, I noticed each had left her daytime clothes hanging on a line strung from one wall peg to a peg on an opposite wall. This was a custom in my country; quite often robes—made dusty during the day—were rinsed out, then hung up to dry during the night.

The idea came to me that I might leave coins in each girl's daytime robe, provided I could find pockets in them. But the room was too poorly lit to see the robes clearly. If I had to fumble around with them looking for pockets, I might knock down the whole clothesline and wake everybody up for certain. I had no sister or other female relative; I wasn't quite sure where pockets were on girls' robes.

But alongside the robes on the clothesline were three pairs of rough wool stockings. Everyone wore these during certain times of the year, sometimes to keep out the cold and other times to avoid burns on our bare legs when the desert winds blew sand about in hard, scratchy clouds. The stockings were obviously sturdy. Within seconds, I'd put four silver coins in each pair—two coins in each stocking. The girls couldn't help but discover the money when they woke in the morning and started to dress.

Thrilled to have given my gifts, I inched back across the room, grabbed my ladder, and leaned it back up toward the window. I clambered up, balanced on the sill, and pulled up the ladder. As I leaned it back from the windowsill to the street, Sara again began gasping. This time she woke herself up, and her sisters, too. All three sat up, and as they did I hurried a bit too much and the ladder clacked against the windowsill. I just caught a quick glimpse of their pale, startled faces looking up at me before I scurried over the sill and down the ladder, and began hurrying back toward the inn. I expected to hear screams behind me, but it remained quiet. I returned the ladder to the shed, sneaked back to my room, and then lay in my bed awake until dawn, feeling happier than I could ever remember. There's nothing better than giving gifts, I thought over and over.

In the morning the village was full of the news that old Shem's daughters had miraculously received dowries from an unknown stranger who'd somehow gotten into their house during the night to leave his wonderful gifts in their stockings. Almost immediately, it was announced there would be three weddings within the week. Everyone in Patara attended. Phillip wasn't the priest who married the three girls and their suitors, but I noticed during the service that he was looking at me and smiling with pride.

All three of Shem's daughters had long, happy marriages. I swore then and there I would find more opportunities to leave presents and make others happy, always coming in secret during the night.

And that's how my career as a gift-giver began.

"You're nearing sixteen," Phillip told me one day, when I'd come
to report another successful gift-giving trip, this one to the children
of some nomads in a desert camp to the northwest.
"You're now a man, and a man has to make some decisions."

TWO

Nicholas, Bishop

t first I confined my gift-giving to Patara. Every hungry family received money for food, every ragged family got money for clothing. This money was always left with children, so their parents would not feel ashamed. Mostly, I visited houses, although sometimes I sneaked into tents if that was where need existed. I always gave my gifts in secret and at night. Not every night, of course, but once or twice every month.

However, I soon found that my simple plan had to be changed. By the time I'd been making my after-dark excursions for six months, everyone in the village knew some mysterious benefactor was entering homes at night and leaving money as a sign of his visit. Some greedy people who hoped to be next began sitting up nights, and sleeping during the day. A few went so far as to spend dusk until dawn in front of their houses hoping to spot the unknown gift-giver passing by, and to convince him to leave his coins for them, whether they really needed the money or not. Too many eyes were watching; I could no longer leave the inn and do my good deeds in secret.

I was frustrated. I consulted Phillip, who said I should simply think about it until a solution presented itself. Soon enough, it did. One evening at the inn I overheard a merchant who was staying overnight talk about a poor teenager in nearby Myra. This girl's legs had been weak from birth. She lived with her mother, who considered her to be a useless burden. A dressmaker in the young girl's town wanted to hire her to keep customer accounts, but, despite her spirit and intelligence, she could not walk from her home to the dressmaker's shop. If she had a stout pair of crutches, however, the girl could manage the short journey. But charity was scarce in Myra, and no one would buy the crutches for her.

"It's time to take my presents to other places," I told Phillip. "I'll go the twenty miles to Myra and leave money in the girl's stocking. Then she can buy her crutches, go to work for the dressmaker, and have a chance for a better life."

Phillip said it was a noble plan, and so that day I borrowed a mule from the inn's stable, telling the man who worked there that I wanted to visit a friend in Myra. I departed early in the morning and arrived just at dusk.

Discreet inquiries helped me learn where the girl lived—in a dirty, one-room house that looked to me like it was infested with spiders and mice. Still, it was easy enough to enter unnoticed after she and her mother were asleep. I left the money in the girl's stocking, took a room at the nearby inn, and allowed myself the pleasure the next morning of waiting to see the girl buy her crutches and begin her new life. But the girl's mother took the money from her, and spent it on herself while her daughter remained helpless at home.

"That mother needs to be punished," I complained to Phillip after returning home to Patara. "She's evil to deprive her daughter that way."

As always, my friend the priest was wiser than I. "It's not your place to assign blame, Nicholas," he said sternly. "Perhaps the greatest fault was with your plan, rather than with the mother. Did you leave a note with the coins, saying the money was to be used for crutches? No? I thought not."

"I know that woman would have ignored such a note," I said peevishly. "Writing it would have been a waste of my time. If you know a way I could have done better, why don't you tell me? I'm tired from the trip and I don't feel like guessing."

Phillip shrugged, "The answer seems simple enough to me. The girl can't walk from her home to the dressmaker's shop leaning on coins. If she needs crutches, give her crutches. Her mother can't spend those."

He was right, of course. I went to the market in Patara to buy crutches, only to learn none were available. Well, I had some basic skill at carving wood. I simply found a tree with proper-sized branches, cut two down, and trimmed them to the right shape. To make the gift more special, I removed the bark from the branches and spent the better part of a week carving intricate designs into the wood—birds and flowers and people with happy, smiling faces to remind the girl there was goodness in the world.

When the crutches were ready, I rode the mule back to Myra, waited until dark, entered the girl's house, and silently laid the crutches by her sleeping mat. I wasn't able to stay the next morning to see what happened next, but a few weeks later the merchant from whom I had first heard the girl's story returned to our inn and told how she had begun working for the dressmaker. Two months later the story took an even happier turn; feeling proud that her crippled daughter had done so well, the mother also took proper work. Together, mother and daughter earned enough money to move to a better, cleaner house.

I took heart from the experience. At night at the inn I made it my business to listen to the guests as they gossiped over dinner, telling stories about nearby villages and residents there in need. As often as possible, when I heard that someone needed help, I tried to provide it. Occasionally, I'd still leave money with children, but more often now I'd leave warm cloaks for a family in rags, or sandals for parents and children so poor they had to go around barefoot.

As my adventures spread farther and farther from my home village, so did the tale of the mysterious benefactor who left nighttime gifts. As usual, the stories far surpassed fact. I never was able to get much more than fifty miles from home, but myth had it that I'd made visits as far away as the far northern coast. There was immediate benefit; the greedy citizens of Patara stopped watching out for me every night, and I was once again able to make occasional stops in my own hometown.

Yet I still wasn't satisfied. Rumor had me traveling most of the known world, from Rome to Jerusalem and back again. Rumor or not, the thought intrigued me. My desire to give was unrestricted by borders between countries. I had the money to book passage by ship or wagon train to almost anywhere, and that is how I thought I'd spend my adult life. But, as usual, Phillip found a flaw in my plan.

"You're nearing sixteen," he told me one day, when I'd come to report another successful gift-giving trip, this one to the children of some nomads in a desert camp to the northwest. "You're now a man, and a man has to make some decisions. You need a profession. Otherwise, you'll gain a reputation as a wealthy, lazy fool. Besides, no matter what good deeds you do at night, you need an honest job for the daytime hours, if only so you'll better appreciate what other men and women do to earn their daily bread."

I hadn't thought about much of anything beyond giving gifts at night. Truly, I didn't mind the idea of finding a profession. The few people who'd inherited enough wealth to sit home all day were mocked by everybody else, and rightly so. There's nothing wrong with hard, honest work.

"What should I do?" I asked Phillip.

He replied that I ought to consider my interests and find a job where the work would be both enjoyable to me and helpful to the community.

"I'd like to travel more," I said. "Maybe I could invest some of my money in merchandise and open shops in all the civilized cities."

"Suppose your investments were bad and you lost all your money?" he replied. "How would you give your gifts then?"

Phillip smiled when he said this, so I knew he believed he had a solution. I must have spent ten minutes guessing before he finally said what was on his mind. "Why not become a priest? We're supposed to be poor, it's true, but the money you inherited would still be yours outside of the church. You could do good deeds by day as a priest and by night you could continue your other adventures. Besides, nobody finds out more about those in need than a priest."

I agreed immediately, although I knew the life I was choosing would be difficult. It was a harsh world then, as I suppose it still is today, but Christians might have been among the people who suffered most. Rome still ruled most of the known world (there were, of course, other countries and cultures, such as China, that dominated other parts of the Earth; those people knew as little of us then as we knew of them). There seemed to be a new Roman emperor every few years, and each had his own opinion about Christians. Some let us live in peace; others ordered terrible persecutions, starting with a man named Nero, who blamed us for burning down part of Rome, although no Christians were involved. Other religions were much more established than the Christian Church, which was still very, very new. Not long before my birth in 280 A.D., for instance, a Roman emperor named Aurelian worshiped Sol Invictus, a sun god, and that became the official religion of Rome.

The Christian Church itself had problems. Some of its leaders lived in Rome and had one idea of what the church should be like; there was another powerful group of leaders in Antioch who thought they were right about everything. Stuck in the middle were the bishops in charge of different regions and the priests who served in villages. Between Roman emperors and their own church leaders, Christians had to endure confusing times.

I always believed the whole purpose of being a Christian was to do good things for those in need, and so I chose to think about that and not about the negative aspects of becoming a priest. Phillip thought I should begin my career by going to Alexandria, in Egypt, where there was a school for priests. One of the school's first teachers had been a man named Origen, whom I admired for translating parts of the Old Testament into different languages so that more people could read them. Origen died thirty years before I was born, but his school was still open.

I said good-bye to my friends in Patara and sailed to Alexandria, excited about my new adventure. Very few people in my hometown could read, so it was especially enjoyable to be with other students who loved books.

Alexandria was the biggest city I'd ever seen. It had libraries and wonderful statues and marketplaces offering for sale everything I could imagine and many things I couldn't. The teachers at the school warned us not to wander around the street too much. They insisted we should concentrate on our studies. But I found I could study hard and still explore the city by night. I enjoyed meeting people from other cultures and listening to them talk about their customs. They, in turn, were curious about Christianity. I had many interesting discussions.

I also learned that the bigger the city, the greater the number of people in need. In Alexandria, I saw slums for the first time. Entire neighborhoods of poor people were always hungry, sick, and dirty. When my schedule permitted, I made some gift-giving trips, although when I did I was always saddened to think that for every child I helped, hundreds of others were still doing without.

It also was at school in Alexandria that I first gave much thought to something very important—how to celebrate the birth of Jesus. The teachers told us it shouldn't be celebrated at all, that we would insult Jesus if we celebrated his birthday as though he were just another human being. Origen in particular had believed that. It was one of the arguments dividing the church. Despite what Origen believed and preached, many Christians celebrated Jesus' birth anyway, usually on January 6. They'd have a feast and sing songs in his honor. I'd never seen anything wrong with this. In fact, on that day I usually brought cheese, bread, and wine to share with Phillip and the other priests of Patara.

After listening to my teachers in Alexandria, I still believed Origen was wrong. I was young enough to be very stubborn. I decided that I would find ways to celebrate Jesus' birthday with as many others as possible. There's nothing wrong with happiness.

I studied in Alexandria for almost two years. Despite our differences of beliefs regarding Jesus' birthday, the teachers decided I had learned enough to go out into the world as a priest. I wanted to travel to as many faraway places as possible, but felt I should start my new life back in my home country. I wanted to see Phillip again, and was anxious to get back to my old routine of giving gifts.

The place in Patara where Phillip and the other priests lived was called a monastery. I lived with them there for a year, and when I was nineteen they honored me by electing me abbot, or leader, after the old abbot passed away. Three years later the area's bishop also died, and I was elected to replace him. At age twenty-two, I was the church leader for all Christians in Lycia.

"I don't want to be bishop," I told Phillip one day. I'd had to move out of the monastery in Patara and into a fancy house in Myra, where the bishop was expected to make his home. "I have to spend too much time meeting with other bishops, arguing about church laws. I just want to give presents to children. That's my real interest."

Phillip coughed before answering. Lately, he'd begun looking frail, and that worried me.

"Nicholas, I respect you as my bishop. But I'm tired of constantly hearing you say you want to give up every time things get hard," he said. "Life will always be hard. You chose to become a priest, and you accepted when you were elected bishop. No one made you do these things. Well, I'm a tired old man. Give up, if you must. Otherwise, promise me that from now on you'll complete everything you start, and that no matter how hard something is, you'll have the courage to do whatever is necessary. I'm going to die soon, Nicholas, and you won't have me here anymore to talk you out of giving up."

I cried out of shame for my weakness and at the thought Phillip wouldn't live forever.

"I need you, Phillip," I sobbed. "I can't manage without you."

He smiled. "Everyone has his place in this world, Nicholas, and work to do before leaving it. Somehow, I think you were my work. Keep me in your heart and in your memory. And keep doing the work you were meant to do."

"Do you mean my work with the church, or my work with giving gifts?" I asked.

Phillip just smiled. He never did answer me, but that was his way. He always believed people were better off figuring things out for themselves. When he died a few weeks later, I swore I'd honor him by being the best bishop, and the best gift-giver, who ever lived.

On the night of December 6, 343 A.D.—in my sixty-third year,
if you're counting—I gathered a few things together in a pack,
including my red bishop's robe, picked up the staff,
saddled a mule, and rode quietly off to the north.

THREE

Leaving Home

hat last chapter was rather sad, wasn't it? Well, please don't be unhappy. In that chapter and in this one, I'm telling about the days when I was still a very young man, growing in mind as well as in body. Growing up is never really easy, and we often learn our best lessons from the mistakes we make when we are young. The trick is to learn from those mistakes and go on; this is what I did.

After Phillip was buried, I went back to my house in Myra and did my best to fulfill my promises to him. I worked very hard, during the day as bishop and at night as the mysterious gift-giver. In some ways I was able to keep the two jobs separate. Bishops always had to settle disputes, some having nothing at all to do with the church. If two neighboring farmers couldn't decide the right dividing line between their properties, for instance, they might come and ask me to pray about it until God told me the answer. I always believed God had more important things to attend to, so usually I'd go out and see the situation for myself, then suggest a compromise. Most often they'd accept whatever I suggested, and afterward there might be a feast to celebrate their agreement. Bishops attended lots of feasts. I began to gain some weight.

Nights usually found me giving my gifts. As bishop, I had to travel, and if, for instance, I visited the small village of Niobrara and heard of a boy there who needed sandals, after my next overnight visit to that town he'd wake in the morning to find the sandals beside his sleeping mat. I was almost always able to get in and out without being seen; the few times I was glimpsed at all, it was by children or parents so foggy with sleep that they couldn't be sure they weren't dreaming.

It was inevitable, though, that descriptions of the mysterious night-time gift-giver would emerge. I was variously described as short and tall, stout and thin, old and young, bearded and clean-shaven. I was said to be able to turn myself into mist and float into houses through cracks in doorways, or else able to fly from one place to another. The few hints I might be a demon were quickly hooted down. After all, it was immediately pointed out, I only gave good gifts, while a demon would prefer causing pain to bringing joy.

One portion of my description was usually the same, and properly so. The gift-giver was almost always described as wearing red robes with white trimming on the collar and sleeves. Well, as bishop I was usually required to wear the red robes with white trim that signified my office. More often than not, I was unable to pack other clothing for my trips, so I wore what I already had on when I sneaked off at night to give gifts.

You might wonder why, if the gift-giver and the bishop wore the same clothing, someone didn't use this obvious clue to solve the mystery and announce we were one and the same. Also, no one ever wondered aloud why the gift-giver always left his presents in the same villages where the bishop had just visited. Well, here's my conclusion, based on nearly two thousand years of observing human nature: People look, but they don't always know what they're seeing.

I must admit that sometimes my responsibilities as bishop interfered with my gift-giving. There were endless conferences to attend, where bishops from all over argued about points I personally found insignificant. When my turn came to speak, I'd always say I thought we could better spend our time helping the poor instead of debating issues that couldn't really be resolved anyway. As a result, I was not especially popular among my fellow bishops.

Please don't get the idea that I had no respect for the church, or that I always put gift-giving ahead of Christianity. Once I was even put in prison for more than a year; the Roman Emperor Diocletian had ordered all Christians to worship gods other than their own. I chose to go to prison rather than obey. I sat in a cell until that emperor died. Another took his place and allowed Christians to again worship as they pleased.

When I got out of prison, I was amazed to hear that, according to gossip, the gift-giver hadn't interrupted his services while Bishop Nicholas of Myra was otherwise detained. At first I thought these stories were all made up. In fact, many were. But upon further investigation I was pleased to find that, in a few cases, others had decided to imitate me and give presents to children in need. Instead of taking credit, they let everyone think it was the work of the original gift-giver. Being kind is its own reward.

The new century, called the fourth but including all the years numbered in the three hundreds, began badly for Christians in

303 A.D., when the emperor made new, harsh rules for us. But the Roman Empire was dividing under its own sheer size and population. For a while it was split into two empires, West and East, with each half ruled by a co-emperor. Eventually Constantine I, often called Constantine the Great in history books, took complete control. Constantine became a Christian himself, and gradually our church became the recognized religion of the empire, although this took some time. At first it was sufficient to know we could openly practice Christianity without fear of being thrown in jail or even put to death.

I took advantage of this new freedom to travel even more widely. Wherever I went, I tried to present religion as a cause for joy and not a source of fear. "Help each other the way you would want God to help you," I said over and over. To borrow a phrase, I practiced what I preached. The church had wealth, if not in coins then in rich farmlands, and I ordered the food grown on these lands to be given to the poor. Sick people were often shunned by those who were healthy. To set a good example, I would go to the sick in each town I visited, bringing them nourishing soup and bathing their heads with cool water. Many times, in those days, sick people simply died because they were ignored. After a few I visited regained their health, they began to tell others that I saved them through miracles, though I'd really done nothing of the sort. Others, fed when I ordered church farmland used for their benefit, began claiming I had called the food up out of thin air. Most people then weren't well educated, of course, and it was a time when most reported miracles were accepted as fact. That was certainly true of the stories involving me.

My new fame became a terrible burden. Wherever I went, people came up to me asking to be healed or fed. I did what I could, but there were limits to my abilities. Yet more and more often, people seemed to believe I could do anything if I really wanted. They began camping outside my door at night, ready to beg me to do impossible things the moment I stepped outside. Of course, this prevented me from doing any nighttime gift-giving. I hoped the myths about me would go away after a while, but they didn't. Instead, they spread farther and attracted more hopeful sufferers to my door. I had never felt so frustrated, by both the expectations of others and my own inability to do what they wanted.

For months, I tried to think of what I should do. The more people expected of me, the less I could actually do to help them. It was terribly frustrating. Then one night I had a dream. Phillip was in it, seeming as real as though he were right there with me. He said, "Nicholas, be brave just a little while longer. Get your church in order and wait for another dream, because there's a solution to your problems."

So I kept trying to do the best I could to cope with the demands on me. Every day started with requests for help and ended the same way. Days turned into weeks, weeks into years. I noticed everyone else around me growing old; I was doing the same. My hair began to turn white, and so did my beard. I neared my sixty-third birthday and assumed most of my life was over. Then the second dream came.

I see my mirror image

Phillip was in it again, of course. He told me to get up and look in the mirror. Whether I really did this or only dreamed I did, I can't say. But there was the mirror, and there was my reflection in it, and Phillip said, "Remember every line and wrinkle, because you will not grow any older."

"Then I'm going to die now," I answered, not really afraid of the idea at all.

Phillip laughed, the same dry chuckle I'd heard so often when I was a child and had just asked him a foolish question. "No, Nicholas. Your life so far is just a single grain of sand in an hourglass. It is only beginning."

"That can't be," I protested. "I'm nearly sixty-three years old. No one lives much longer than that."

"Remember this, Nicholas," Phillip said. "Time is different for each of us; a year to one man is one hundred years to another. Stop worrying about the end of life. Now it's time for you to start your gift-giving again."

"The people won't let me," I argued. "They stay outside my door. They follow me wherever I go."

"You haven't changed since you were a boy," Phillip said, not sounding especially pleased at the thought. "The simple solutions are always best. Just go."

Then the dream was over, if it really was a dream. I was sitting up in bed, with the words "Just go" echoing in my mind. I didn't go that night, though. I spent the next few days visiting with various bankers in Myra and Patara, bringing my financial affairs up to date and gathering the remaining money from my parents' estate. This was not an unusual thing for an old man to do. Word spread that Bishop Nicholas was settling accounts; obviously he felt he was about to die. Some of the supplicants surrounding my house respected this and went away, often calling back over their shoulders that they'd pray for my soul if I'd only work a few last miracles for them.

Beyond getting my finances together, I made no real plans. On the night of December 6, 343 A.D.—in my sixty-third year, if you're counting—I gathered a few things together in a pack, including my red bishop's robe, picked up a staff, saddled a mule, and rode quietly off to the north. I chose to go north because it seemed the right direction at the time. I had no idea what would happen to me next, but I believed I was part of some higher power's plan. This belief seemed to light my way as I ventured into the darkness and whatever future it might hold for me.

The Romans were people who enjoyed parties. During Saturnalia all stores were closed down, except the ones selling food and wine. It became the Roman custom to give gifts to family members and friends at this time, not big things, but items such as candy, cake, and fruit.

FOUR

Why the Calendar Changed

et's leave me heading north into the night for a bit. Even as I started my journey into the unknown, there were other things happening in the world, things that greatly affected my future.

The most important were changes involving the way Christians celebrated Jesus' birthday. Despite Origen doing his best to prevent it, many people chose to honor Jesus' birth with special meals, songs, or other ways to show how happy they were that he had been born on this Earth. But not everyone celebrated on the same date. Many chose January 6, but others preferred December 25. No one knew the exact date Jesus was born, so one guess was as good as another.

The first recorded December 25 celebration was in Antioch, in the middle of the second century. Some priests and members of the church there had a feast in honor of the occasion. They tried not to be too noticeable when they did it—Christians were being persecuted at the time. There were few of these celebrations for another hundred years or so. It was a real risk to have one. After Roman Emperor Constantine became a Christian, though, a lot of people in the church could openly express their joy by making their celebrations of Jesus' birth into elaborate festivities. Some of these celebrations lasted several days; all included lots of good food and drink.

(By the way, have you noticed I'm using phrases such as "celebration of Jesus' birth," but never "Christmas," the name you probably expect? That's because the word "Christmas" wasn't being used yet. It wouldn't be for quite some time. The same thing is true for "Santa Claus." For many centuries to come, I would still be known as Nicholas.)

Although Constantine had embraced Christianity, there wasn't an official holiday honoring Jesus' birthday at the time of my departure from Myra. That official recognition came seven years later, in 350 A.D., when Pope Julius I—who was head of the church in Rome—formally declared that December 25 would be celebrated each year as Jesus' birthday. Julius was late in making this announcement. Roman records already had noted a "nativity feast" on December 25 as an annual event going back as far as 336 A.D.

It's interesting how the Romans chose December 25 as the correct date. For hundreds of years, Rome was the greatest military power on Earth, and its armies were constantly fighting to extend the boundaries of the Roman Empire farther in every direction, especially into what would become northern and western Europe and the islands beyond (which were eventually named Britain).

Rome almost always imposed its own laws on nations it conquered, but sometimes Romans also absorbed some of the customs of the countries they defeated, especially in matters of religion.

Religion was important to the Romans, but they changed faiths like modern-day people change clothes. When Rome conquered Greece, for instance, they adopted the Greek gods, giving them new names, but essentially keeping the same ideas about them. Like lots of other pre-Christians, the Greeks celebrated something we now call winter solstice, or the time of year when the daylight hours are shortest and the weather turns cold. In ancient times, winter meant crops couldn't be grown and people had to live on whatever food they'd stored up during the harvest. To please the gods, and to convince them to bring back warmer weather, people in many different civilizations, both before and after the Roman Empire existed, would have feasts during the solstice, offering gifts to the gods as bribes to make the crop-growing seasons return.

One of the Greek gods was renamed "Saturn" by the Romans, who called their new solstice celebration "Saturnalia" in his honor. It was a long celebration, lasting from December 17 to December 24. The Romans were people who enjoyed parties. During Saturnalia all stores were closed down, except the ones selling food and wine. It became the Roman custom to give gifts to family members and friends at this time, not big things, but items such as candy, cake, and fruit.

Then along came Emperor Aurelian, whom we've talked about before. Aurelian wanted to worship Persian sun gods, and made his people do the same. They didn't really argue much; it certainly wasn't the first time Rome's official religion was changed, though it would only happen once more with Constantine. Aurelian proclaimed **"Dies Invicta Solis,"** or "Day of the Invincible Sun," on December 25. He did this because Mithra, the Persian god of light, was supposed to have been born on that day. His religion was known as Mithraism. Constantine believed in that faith until he became a

Christian. When he did, he changed December 25 from a day of celebrating Mithra's birth to a day of celebrating Jesus' birth instead. As long as the Roman people got their day of feasting, I don't suppose most of them really cared whose birthday they celebrated.

In the centuries since, some people who don't like Christmas have criticized the holiday for its date, saying quite truthfully that it's almost certain Jesus wasn't born on December 25, during the winter. Scholars studying the Bible think it's likely he was born sometime during the spring, instead. To me, the specific date of Jesus' birth is less important than the fact that he was born at all, and that lots of people want to celebrate his birth. As you'll learn later on, December 25 is just one of the days on which I do my yearly gift-giving. Children in some countries expect me on December 6, my name day, and others on January 6, which is officially called Epiphany. In some countries, January 6 is thought to be the date that the Wise Men finally arrived in Bethlehem and gave their gifts to the baby Jesus.

All this is fine with me. It's the spirit of the season, being generous to others who don't have much and being grateful for the things we have, that really matters. Dates are, after all, just names and numbers made up by people long, long ago.

The first Roman calendar is supposed to have been introduced in 738 B.C. It had ten months and lasted 304 days. The names of some of its months ought to sound familiar to you: Martius, Aprilis, Maius, Junius, Quintilis, Sextilis, September, October, November, and December. The last six names are taken from the Roman words for five, six, seven, eight, nine, and ten.

That calendar was invented by Romulus, the first ruler of Rome. One of his descendants, Numa Pompilius, added the months of January and February, which made the Roman year 355 days long. If Pompilius had stopped there it would have been best, but then he got the idea of adding an extra month every other year. Within a few years, winter was arriving in September instead of November and December.

Which day was what got so mixed up that 46 B.C. was known as the Year of Confusion. Julius Caesar was emperor then, and he commanded that the calendar somehow be fixed. The solution was to make 46 B.C. 445 days long to get the seasons back to the right months. In his honor, the month of Quintilis was renamed July. Later on, Sextilis became August in honor of Caesar Augustus.

This new order, called the Julian calendar, was used for the next fifteen hundred years. But it still wasn't quite accurate. By 1580, the calendar and the people who used it were ten days off.

In 1582, Pope Gregory decided it was time for another calendar change. For that year, he ordered the ten extra days taken out of October, and then worked out what eventually became a complicated plan to add one extra day in February every fourth year, just to keep everything exactly in line. Some countries took a long time to agree to these changes. Russia didn't start using the Gregorian calendar until 1918, and it was 1927 before Turkey did.

I tell this to point out why it's obvious we can't ever be certain what date things happened around the time of Jesus' birth. Picking one day is as good as picking any other. I have enough trouble remembering the names of my friends at the North Pole, or Layla's and my wedding anniversary. As far as I'm concerned, people who argue that Christmas is all wrong because it's celebrated on December 25 should use their energy to help needy people instead. That's the best way to celebrate anything.

Anyway, making December 25 an official feast day was just one important step for the Christian church following Constantine's conversion. For the first time, it also was possible for many priests to travel about telling the story of Jesus without fear of being thrown in prison, tortured, or even killed. One of the big advantages Rome brought to nations it conquered was the constant building of roads, very good ones, some of which have lasted to this day. You can go to certain places in Europe and Britain and actually walk or drive on roads originally built by the Romans. Although they were fierce fighters, you see, Romans really wanted to control the world through trading. Roman merchants needed roads to move their goods from one market to another. These roads also came in handy for priests and other Christians who wanted to walk or ride long distances. All along the way, the mighty soldiers of Rome would now protect them from harm instead of hurting them. It made a big difference!

Of course, Christianity has lasted much longer than the Roman Empire, which began to crumble in the fifth century. Much to my amazement, I lasted longer than the Romans, too.

"It's obvious you're a thief who wants to knock me over the head and steal my money, if I have any money. You're not even a good thief, either. Look—I can see that stick you're hiding behind your back. You hope to hit me with it."

FIVE

The Beginning
of Magic

his is the part of my story where the magic begins. There will be more magic times to come, but I'm going to tell you now about the first. Remember what we discussed earlier: Illusion can be explained, magic can't. So far, my adventures in gift-giving had been colored with illusion. I quietly entered people's homes and left gifts for their children. Because of this, they created myths about me being able to fly or to turn myself into the wind and blow inside. Yet I got in by using ladders or opening doors, nothing more special than that.

But I expect you're eager to hear about the magic now, so let's resume my tale.

After leaving my home behind, I kept traveling north and west from Myra. Sometimes I rode the mule, but not very often. I would have soon become tired of carrying him on my back, and I assumed he felt the same about me. I had left no family behind and had none ahead, so the mule was the closest thing I had to a relative. I named him "Uncle" and amused myself by talking to him along lonely stretches of road.

Since the Romans had built good roads, there were many other travelers along my route. I was going in the general direction of Constantinople, with the idea of getting ship passage from there to Rome. This wasn't unusual. Lots of tourists wanted to see the sights there—the Coliseum, the Appian Way, the Senate where the government conducted business, and so forth. I knew I wouldn't mind looking at these places and things if I happened to find myself standing in front of them, but I was going to Rome for a different purpose—because I had a feeling it was the next place I should be.

It was going to be a long walk before I reached Constantinople, hundreds of miles, and as a sixty-three-year-old man I expected I would tire easily. This didn't happen. I would walk all day and then walk through the night hours, and when the sun came up again I'd find I had walked thirty miles, or even forty or fifty. This was impossible; in one day at normal speed I might have been able to travel twenty miles if I rode the mule part of the way. My steps weren't longer than any other man's. I'd always needed as much sleep as anyone else. Yet somehow I was walking farther in one day than any man ever had, and still I wasn't feeling tired, although I rarely slept at all. In five days I was in Constantinople. The journey should have taken two weeks. This was the first magic. It wasn't anything spectacular like being able to fly, but there was no way to logically explain it. Somehow, as I walked, time and distance became different for me than for everybody else.

It was easy to get a berth on a ship to Rome. Merchant vessels let travelers pay for the privilege of sleeping in their holds along with

Constantinople and Rome

whatever goods were being shipped. Some people would only sail on ships carrying cargos of aromatic spices or fresh-smelling linens. Although I wasn't sure why, I wanted to get to Rome as quickly as possible, so I paid to board the first ship sailing there from Constantinople. It was a cattle ship. The animals bellowed constantly. I didn't mind. I'd grown fond of Uncle the mule and was pleased to be able to take him to Rome with me. He was tethered down in the hold with hay to eat. I spent the twelve-day voyage on deck, enjoying the sea air and idly wondering what I was going to do when we arrived.

The other passengers were all seasick for the first few days. As for me, I never felt a twinge of discomfort. Indeed, I heartily ate all the food the crew offered me, and they offered a lot in hopes I'd get an upset stomach and turn green like the rest of the passengers. It was a game the sailors liked to play. When I consumed cheese and bread and jelly and fruit and candy and fish, and didn't lose my meal overboard right afterward, the sailors clapped me on the back and invited me to their cabin area to sing songs with them. When they asked my name, I said it was Nicholas. They were all strangers and I didn't think they'd know about a humble bishop from Myra.

"Say, you're named the same as that bishop who works miracles down in Lycia!" one of the crewmen boomed out.

Well, so much for that. Before I could say a word, the other sailors chimed in with stories they'd heard about the wonderful Bishop Nicholas, how he'd touched one finger to a blind man's eyes and made him see again, and how he'd planted a single grain of wheat in the ground and stalks sprouted for acres in every direction. They were very entertaining stories. I could even enjoy them, if I forgot they were supposed to be about me.

My mule, "Uncle"

"On my next shore leave I intend to go to that bishop's town, Myra, I think it's called, and see him work some of these miracles for myself," a sailor said.

"Would you be very disappointed if this bishop turned out to be an ordinary man who worked no miracles at all?" I asked.

"Don't be so sour," he urged me. "Don't you think that, in this hard world, we all need some magic to believe in?"

He was right, of course. That night, for the first time since I'd left Myra, I curled up in a blanket and tried to sleep until dawn. I hoped I'd dream again about Phillip, and that he'd tell me something more about time standing still. Instead, I dreamed about snow, something I'd not seen in Lycia but had heard about—frozen rain coming down from the sky and turning into a soft white blanket over the Earth. When I awoke the next morning, I thought it was odd to have dreamed of such a thing.

When we docked in Rome, I found it to be the biggest, loudest, dirtiest place that ever could have existed. Most streets were paved and had gutters, but people washed many disgusting things down those gutters. The city seemed to stretch on forever. It was built on hills, and every hill was covered with buildings.

The winter cold was fierce. I used a little of my money to buy warmer clothes. Now that I'd arrived, I wondered what I should do next. On an impulse, I took a room at a small inn. At dinnertime, I went downstairs, ordered a simple meal of bread and cheese, and sat at a table to eat it. When I was done, I put on my new heavy cloak and walked outside.

"You! Yes, you!" hissed a voice from the shadows. "Come over here. I've got an important message for you!"

I looked, and there in an alley beside the inn was a scared-looking stout man. His round face was dirty and, though it was so cold, his forehead was shining with sweat.

"What do you mean, a message?" I asked. "No one in this city knows who I am, or even that I'm here."

"I was told to give you a message," the man insisted. "Won't you come and get it from me?"

"Certainly not," I said. "It's obvious you're a thief who wants to knock me over the head and steal my money, if I have any money. You're not even a good thief, either. Look—I can see that stick you're hiding behind your back. You hope to hit me with it."

The fellow looked behind himself and said, "A stick? What stick? Oh, that one? I've never seen it before. Someone must have put it in my hand. Please come and get your message. I'm very hungry."

"Why should my getting a message have anything to do with your hunger?" I asked. "This is a silly conversation. You want to rob me and I don't want to be robbed. I believe you must be the worst thief in the world, to be so obvious about it. You should be ashamed of planning to hit an innocent stranger over the head with your stick."

The man dropped the stick and took a few steps forward. I could see his clothes were torn and not heavy enough to keep out the cold.

"I'm sorry," he muttered. "I wasn't really going to hit you, anyway. I just wanted you to think I'd hit you if you didn't give me your money. I could never hurt anyone. That's why I'm so hungry now."

He didn't seem very dangerous, just sad.

"Why is that?" I asked. "Tell me your story. But first, why don't we go back inside the inn, where it's warm? I'll gladly buy you dinner. There's no need to rob me if you need money for a meal."

The would-be thief looked so grateful that I knew I'd said the right thing.

We went back inside the inn, and I told him to order all the food he wanted. At first I think he didn't believe I would pay for his meal, and asked for water and bread, the very cheapest things. So I pulled out a coin, big enough to pay for all the food in the kitchen, and soon my new companion was gobbling away from a mountain of meat, cheese, and pastry.

"You're a fat fellow to be starving," I noted. "I mean no offense, but how come you're so hungry? When did you eat last?"

"At midday," he said between huge bites on a leg of lamb. He held the meat in his hands; no one used knives and forks back then. "I can't help it. I just need more food than most. I've been stealing my meals for a week, ever since I ran away from my master."

He lowered his voice when he said this. Slavery was part of Roman society, and runaway slaves were severely punished whenever they were caught.

"Did your master beat you?" I asked. "Were you in fear for your safety?"

"I was in fear for my own life and the lives of others," he said. "My master said I ate too much, and ordered me to train as a wrestler. He meant to make me fight other wrestlers, and charge admission to watch. Well, I don't like other people hurting me, and I don't like hurting other people. So I ran away."

"Don't you miss your family?" I wondered. "Don't you miss your friends?"

"I have no family or friends," he replied, and his answer touched my heart. I quickly sensed he was a good person, and I admired him for running away from a master who wanted him to fight.

"Well, now you have a friend," I said. "My name is Nicholas. I'm alone, as well. I'm not sure where I'm going or what I'm doing next, but I have one plan you might like. I have some money. Why don't I go see your master and ask if I can buy you? Since I hate slavery, I'll set you free right away, and you can go wherever you like and not have to fight anyone."

Felix

Tears of joy filled the man's eyes. "Would you really do that?" he asked. "Are you sure this isn't a trick to learn my master's name and then take me back to him? I suppose he's offering some kind of reward for me."

"You have my word on it," I promised. "Let's get some sleep tonight, and in the morning we'll find your master and make everything right."

I paid the innkeeper a little extra to let the man sleep in my room with me. I would have gotten him his own room, but I thought he still might worry during the night that I really meant to trick him and force him back into slavery, and that might make him decide to run away before dawn. It wasn't until he was rolling himself up in the clean linen bedding that I remembered to ask him, "What's your name?"

"I'm Felix," he said. Then, before he could finish a huge yawn, he fell fast asleep.

Felix must have been very tired from running away and hiding. He snored loudly most of the night, but I was used to the cattle mooing on the boat and the noise didn't disturb me.

In the morning we went to see Felix's master, a mean old man who wanted to beat Felix for running away as an example to his other slaves. But I offered a great deal of money if he would sell me Felix instead, and unbeaten.

"Give me the money and make the sale official before I tell you this," the nasty old slaveowner growled. I gave him the coins and he snatched them from my hand, carefully tucking them into his purse before saying, "You've bought a useless slave. He eats too much and has too kind a heart."

"As of this moment, he's not a slave at all," I answered. Under Roman law, it was possible for owners to declare their slaves free at any time. "He's now as free as you or me." Felix, standing beside me, yelped with happiness.

His former owner cringed. "Don't let him near me! He'll attack me because of the way I treated him!"

Before I could reply, Felix said, "Slave or free man, I would never hurt anyone, even you. I do beg you to be nicer to the rest of your slaves, and to consider setting them all free. It's wrong for one human being to own another."

The slaveowner was too greedy to set any of his other slaves free, but at least Felix had asked. Afterward, we walked back to the inn, discussing where we might want to go next since neither of us really liked the crowded streets of Rome. It just seemed completely natural for us to assume we'd stay together. That's how Felix joined me and my next adventures began.

I felt embarrassed when we came to the tomb; it was a grand monument
and I couldn't help thinking how many poor people could have
been helped with the money it took to build it.

SIX

Felix and Me

suspect you didn't think there was enough magic in that last chapter—just being able to walk fast and sometimes not needing to sleep. Well, not all magic is fireworks and fanfare. Sometimes magic is quiet and sneaks up on you. An illusion is what needs all the bells and whistles to make itself appear grander than it really is, which is just a trick that can be explained.

It took Felix and me a while to realize magic was happening to us. We left Rome on foot, leading Uncle the mule. Before leaving the city we bought some provisions, and for the first few weeks of our travels we had a pleasant time exchanging our life stories. Felix was the son of slaves, and his parents were the children of slaves, and beyond that he had no idea of his family roots.

I told Felix all about my gift-giving and being the Bishop of Myra. I wanted to keep on giving my gifts to children, and Felix said right away he hoped to spend the rest of his life helping me do this. So we began to travel about rather aimlessly, finding towns and staying a few weeks while we discovered needy families, then delivering our presents—sandals, perhaps, or cloaks, or, less often, a few coins—during the dark of night and slipping away on the road to the next town before dawn. Mostly we stayed within a hundred miles or so of Rome, although sometimes we ventured into the countries that would later be known as Germany, France, and Spain. There was fighting going on everywhere—Huns and Vandals and Goths and Visigoths and Ostrogoths. Some of those names might sound silly, but the battles were always bitter. The Romans had tried to push the boundaries of their empire too far, and even their mighty legions couldn't fight successfully in so many places at the same time. Meanwhile, ordinary people tried to live their lives as peacefully as possible, keeping their children safe and fed and warm. It was pleasant to think Felix and I helped some of them do this.

We passed many nights gossiping with other travelers around fires at inns where we stopped for the night. It was on one such evening, perhaps a year after Felix and I had begun our travels, that I was stunned to hear a merchant returning home to northern Italy from Lycia tell me the people there had built a wonderful church above the tomb of Nicholas, who'd been Bishop of Myra.

"Tomb?" I asked doubtfully. "What did they put in that tomb?"

The merchant looked at me in wonder. "Why, the bishop's body, of course! What else would be put in a tomb? The man worked wondrous miracles during his life. One night he went into his house to sleep and the next morning they found him lying dead in his bed. So they buried him, and a fine ceremony they apparently made of it."

"Buried him?" I asked, too stunned to say anything more clever.

"People went into the house of Bishop Nicholas and found him there?"

Now the merchant believed he was talking to a very stupid person. "I just said that. They took the body and put it in a great tomb, and then built a great church over that."

"But I——" I began, and Felix poked me in the ribs with his elbow. "I walked away in the middle of the night," I hissed in Felix's ear. "How could they find my body if I was gone?"

Felix and I hurried back to Rome and took passage on a ship to Constantinople. We couldn't find a ship with room for Uncle the mule, so we had to sell him. It was hard to part with such a faithful friend, but I felt his new owner would take good care of him.

We landed safely in Constantinople and walked from there back to Myra. Because I didn't want to be recognized, I camped outside of town and sent Felix ahead. He came back a few hours later shaking his head. "I don't know how to tell you this," he muttered. "You won't believe me."

"I promise I will," I said.

"Well, there is a magnificent church, and inside it is an equally magnificent tomb. This tomb has your name on it, and the date of your death—December sixth, 343 A.D. It even has your likeness carved on marble, although I think you're heavier now than the way they made you look. An old man who was standing beside the tomb said he'd been sleeping outside Bishop Nicholas's door—sorry, outside *your* door—on the fatal night, hoping when you came out the next morning you would heal his leg, which had been crippled from birth. The sun came up, but you didn't come out. By midday people were worried, and it was decided someone should go inside and see if you were all right."

"A crippled man, you say?" I asked. "I really didn't look too

The Roman Empire, as it would appear in the fifth century

closely when I left that night. I tried to step over people quietly so they wouldn't wake up and prevent me from leaving."

Felix's eyebrows knitted together: I was to learn he often had this expression when he was trying especially hard to figure something out. "Well, maybe you didn't get away as completely as you thought. This crippled man was chosen to go inside, and he swears that when he did he found you on your bed, and that you must have died overnight in your sleep. People who had known you for years all agreed the body was yours. It must have resembled you exactly."

"How strange," I said rather faintly. It was odd to hear about someone finding me dead.

"Oh, don't worry, he said everyone mourned you greatly," Felix said quickly, mistaking my bewilderment for disappointment in public reaction. "There were tears all around, and loud wailing, and the decision was made to build you the greatest tomb any bishop ever had."

"How flattering," I muttered.

"Oh, but you haven't heard the best of it," Felix warned. "The tomb was built and the body they found put inside it. Almost at once, this old man told me, a kind of wonderful oil began to drip from the tomb. He got some on his fingers and rubbed it into his crippled leg, which was immediately healed. He pulled up his robes just now to show me how both his legs were strong and healthy."

"This is too strange, Felix," I argued. "I'm sure he never was crippled at all. To find a body when the person hadn't died, and then to say some sort of holy oil seeped from the tomb, well, it's just impossible."

"Perhaps," said Felix, "but you've told me about being able to travel great distances without rest, and that you think time somehow doesn't affect you as it does ordinary men. Where these miracles exist, can't there be others?"

I insisted we go back to town so I could see this tomb for myself. Since I was supposed to be dead, there seemed no danger I'd be recognized, and I wasn't. I passed a few men and women who'd once been my friends, and they never gave me a second glance.

I felt embarrassed as we came to the tomb. It was a grand monument and I couldn't help thinking how many poor people could have been helped with the money it took to build it. No oil was oozing from it, but there were several people kneeling in prayer.

"What are you doing?" I asked one woman.

"Praying to the good Bishop, of course," she replied. "He does miracles for those in need. My daughter is blind. I'm asking the Bishop to restore her sight."

"What if he can't?" I asked.

"Then I'll keep on asking," the woman said. "I know Bishop

Nicholas can't do everything for everyone at once. I'll just keep praying until I get my turn."

I couldn't think of anything else to say. Felix led me away. I was too confused to know where I was going. Eventually, I found myself in an inn that had been built after I'd left Myra. I told Felix I wasn't hungry, and went to our rooms. I immediately fell asleep, and dreamed of a young girl I'd never met who had been blind but suddenly could see. The next day I went back to Nicholas's tomb—my tomb, I suppose— and the woman was gone. Another woman praying nearby said, "Didn't you hear the glad tidings? Someone came running up to her yesterday to say her daughter had regained her sight!"

So I was dead and working miracles. Yet I also was alive and giving my gifts. That, my friends, is magic.

The magic continued. Felix and I left Myra, continuing our journeys and our gift-giving. Days became weeks, weeks became years. One day as we were walking along, Felix stopped short in the middle of the road and said, "Isn't this the year 410?"

"Of course," I said impatiently, for the question seemed foolish. Everyone knew it was 410, a year destined to be remembered as the time Rome was captured and partially destroyed by the Visigoths. The invaders had help; simple peasants and desperate slaves, disgusted with Roman taxes and cruelty, had opened the city gates of Rome from the inside to let the Visigoths enter.

"Well, weren't you sixty-three when we met, and didn't you, uh, change, in the year 343?" Felix wondered.

"You know this as well as I do," I grumbled.

"Well, then, friend Nicholas, doesn't that mean you're now one hundred and thirty?"

I thought about it and added up the years, though addition was never something I did well. "So I am," I finally agreed. "One hundred thirty years old! Tell me, Felix, do I look any different than when we first met?"

He peered at me. "Well, you weigh more."

"Don't be rude."

"Otherwise, you look exactly the same," Felix concluded. "You don't look young, of course. Your hair and beard are white. There are lines in your face and wrinkles around your eyes. But you certainly don't look like someone one hundred and thirty years old, not that anyone could even know what someone that age would look like."

I had attached to my belt a small pouch of personal items, among which was a small circle of polished metal to be used as a mirror. I used it when I trimmed my beard or hair with a small knife. Now, for the first time in a long while, I simply gazed at my reflection.

"See how your face is a bit more puffy from the extra weight," commented Felix, who was watching over my shoulder.

"Worry about your own weight," I snapped, although I knew what Felix said was true. Of course, he himself was shaped like a ball, so I felt he had no right to criticize my few extra pounds. All right, more than a few. But not many more. Ten at the most. With the dignity of my newly discovered years, I decided a man of one hundred thirty was entitled to a wider waistline.

"How wonderful for you," Felix continued, a note of awe in his voice as he considered our discovery. "You're never going to die, ever. You'll be here to watch the world change. Seas will dry up and mountains will crumble, and still you'll be alive to see what happens next. Lucky Nicholas, for some reason you are blessed above all other people!"

It was a sobering thought, and I felt uncomfortable with it. "I really don't think I'll live forever, Felix," I said slowly. "Time might be different for me than others, but it passes all the same. Perhaps a year for me is ten years for someone else, or even a hundred years. Who's to say what this means?"

"I know it means some higher power has special work for you to do on this earth," Felix said firmly. "It must be your gift-giving, for that's the way in which you're most different from ordinary people."

"Yet even when I give gifts I'm left with the feeling I'm not doing all I can and should," I reminded him. "We've talked of this often on our travels. For every child we help, so many more still have to do without. It's a terrible problem."

"Well, it seems you have plenty of time to come up with a solution," Felix replied. "If it's not too much trouble, could you please do this before I, myself, pass on?"

Another thought struck me. "Felix, how old were you when we met back in 343?"

He pondered, "I can't say for certain, Nicholas. The birth dates of slaves weren't always recorded. I suppose I was no longer a very young man, though certainly not much older than—wait! Are you saying what I think you are?"

He rather rudely rummaged in the pouch on my belt, frantic to grab hold of the metal disk and inspect his own reflection.

"Mind your manners!" I protested, slapping his hand away and pulling out the disk myself. "Here! Take a good look, but what you'll see is the same fat face I first encountered in that dark alley outside the Roman inn. You're a bit cleaner now, though still as stout." I couldn't resist this reference to his own poundage. "Let's say you were thirty. No? Is that too old or too young?"

"Too young, I think," Felix said distractedly, twisting the metal mirror this way and that as he peered hard at himself. "I was probably five years older, at least."

"Thirty-five years old, then," I suggested. "Well, add sixty-seven years to it. That would mean you're one hundred and two right now, my fine friend, and though you're not a handsome fellow, you're certainly not wrinkled with such age, either. It would appear that whatever power paused my aging has also chosen to interrupt yours."

"Amazing," Felix said. He sounded stunned, but then he had a right to be. "There was nothing very special about me before I met you—I was just another Roman slave. Do you think this means—?"

"I know," I interrupted. "It means my special mission of gift-giving can't be accomplished alone. I wonder if it's to be just the two of us, Felix, or if we'll be joined by others? Well, I suppose we have plenty of time to find out."

We continued on our way, walking thoughtfully. The packs on our shoulders were heavy. We'd never gotten around to buying a new mule to replace Uncle. Felix lagged a step behind me. After we'd gone perhaps another mile, I heard him say softly, "Nicholas, I'm afraid."

"I'm afraid, too, but I'm also curious," I answered. "Let's give it another century or two, and then maybe things will become more clear."

I woke in the morning to find Felix carving away, and sitting amid a huge
pile of wood shavings. Nine completed planks were stacked beside him, and
he was almost finished with the tenth. Each was beautifully decorated with
carved images that looked real enough to jump off the surface of the wood.

SEVEN

Carving Out
Our Fortunes

ess than a year later we ran out of money. It wasn't a surprise; no personal fortune, however great, could have lasted indefinitely. Although my parents had left me a comfortable amount, it was finally used up between buying the gifts we gave and the simple expenses of living—food, shelter, and clothing of our own. We had just arrived in Constantinople when our last coin was spent, paid to a woman selling apples.

"What do we do now?" asked Felix, crunching his apple loudly. A little juice ran down his chin; my friend never could eat neatly. "What plan do you have to get more money?"

"I have no plan at all," I admitted. "Perhaps you should eat that apple more slowly. It might be your last meal for a while."

It was too late. Felix was already nibbling on the apple core. Carefully tossing it within reach of a camel tethered nearby, he remarked thoughtfully, "So no money means no meals. Well, that's serious. We'd better think of something." And we walked and we pondered, waiting for inspiration.

The plan we needed presented itself in a street market. As we wandered around stalls where all sorts of goods were being sold, we found one merchant surrounded by curious onlookers.

"They're genuine!" he was shouting. "Real copies of the new gospels, copied by the monks of Saint Benedict! If you can read, you'll find the story of Jesus here, and if you can't read, pay someone to read it to you!"

For the last hundred years, copies of so-called "new testaments" had been circulating. It was said that these were written by followers of Jesus to describe Christ's last days on Earth. Most people had heard of these gospels, but few had actually read them. Since each had to be carefully copied by hand, usually by priests, they were quite rare and in great demand among rich people. I had heard stories of churches selling a single copy of one gospel for enough money to support itself for six months.

Curious, Felix and I worked our way through the throng until we stood directly in front of the merchant. He had some parchment papers in his hand, each page covered with elegant handwriting. But the pages themselves weren't as elegant. They were torn in some places and creased along the edges.

"How much for one?" a tall, slender man inquired. He was dressed in wonderful woolen robes dyed bright blue, a tint so expensive only the very rich could afford it.

The merchant, quick to notice those blue robes, named an outrageous price. The rich man laughed and said mockingly, "Look at how your pages are falling apart! Look at the fingerprints made by sweat mixed with ink! And you have the nerve to ask such a high price?"

"What would you pay?" asked the humbled merchant. The rich man named a much lower price, and the sale was concluded. The rest of the crowd still found the new price beyond their means, and so they drifted away.

The merchant unhappily gathered up his remaining copies, preparing to put them in a canvas sack. As he did, and without a word to me, Felix walked up and said cheerfully, "You didn't make much profit on that sale, did you?"

"There was hardly any," the merchant agreed sadly. "The monks drive hard bargains, too. I'm supposed to pick up six more copies of this Gospel of Mark from them next week. I've already paid for those copies, and if I have to sell them at such low prices I won't make enough profit to buy myself a single decent meal."

He and Felix both winced at the thought of missed dinners.

"Well, just protect the pages better," Felix suggested. "If you can keep people from smearing the pages with their fingers and protect the pages from being torn and creased, you should be able to ask a much higher price. Put the pages between covers of wood, like some people in the Roman Empire have done. The wood protects the parchment. The pages remain clean and attractive."

"I like the idea, but I don't know where wood covers could be found on such short notice," the merchant replied. "The monks only make parchment copies. Even if they had the right sort of wood, I don't think any of them have the woodcarving skills to cut and decorate the covers properly."

I listened in amazement as Felix, sounding much like a modern-day salesman, smoothly suggested, "My friend and I can help you.

Give us money to purchase the wood—treated oak is best, I believe, and I know we can find some in this great city—plus a few extra coins as an advance payment for our work. We're woodcarving craftsmen. Then next week we'll present you with six sets of fine wood covers. Take them with you when you get your new parchments from the monks; bind them about the pages and you'll sell every copy as quickly as rich men can pull out their purses and fill your hands with money!"

Felix must have sounded persuasive, because the merchant, whose name was Timothy, agreed almost immediately. He asked only that we first show him the inn where we were staying so he could be certain we wouldn't take his advance payment and run away. We took him there, and the innkeeper confirmed we had already paid for ten days' lodging. I stood watching in amazement as Felix then argued with Timothy over how much more we'd be paid when we brought him his book covers. They finally agreed on a price that, if we really got the money, would pay a month's worth of our traveling expenses and gift-giving costs.

After Timothy left, I asked Felix sharply, "What fix have you gotten us into? If we don't have those covers ready next week, that merchant might have us thrown in prison! Six sets of wooden book covers. Why, it would take both of us a week to carve decorations on one set!"

But Felix didn't seem worried. "Let's go find someone selling the wood we need for the covers," he suggested. "Then I think we need to give ourselves a fine dinner so we'll have the energy to go back to our room and start working."

We found the wood easily enough. We bought twelve small planks of it, two for each set of covers. The planks were heavy, but Felix only carried four of them back to the inn. I had to carry eight. When

I grumbled about having the heavier load, Felix casually told me he needed to save his strength for the job ahead.

After using more of Timothy's money to buy dinner—some roast lamb as well as the usual cheese and bread—we went to our room, pulled out our carving knives, and got to work. The carving was a delicate process. Even a single slip of the knife would mean a whole plank was ruined. As was the custom, we planned to carve stars and angels and elegant patterns on each cover. Some very rich people also decorated their covers with jewels, but we had no jewels. Timothy's customers would have to settle for simple wood.

"I don't think we can do this," I told Felix. "Two men can't carve so much in so little time."

"You've carved a lot of things," he answered. "You're good at it, too. Remember the story you're always telling about the time you gave a little girl a set of crutches? You carved them, didn't you?"

"That was just one set of crutches," I said, but Felix was already bent over a plank. Sighing, I picked up another plank and began pushing the point of my knife blade into the grain of the wood.

We worked for hours. My hands became very tired, and because it was a hot night, sweat began to drip into my eyes. I felt discouraged, but whenever I looked over at Felix he was always carving away, looking very pleased with himself.

Far into the night, I had only carved a small part of one plank. My design was clean and attractive, but there wasn't much of it to admire.

"This is going to be hopeless," I informed Felix. "Tomorrow we'd better seek out Timothy and admit we can't do the job he's paid us to perform. Perhaps he'll give us an extra month or two. After all, the money he gave us is mostly spent, and if he has us thrown in prison he won't ever be able to get it back."

"Oh, are you tired already?" Felix asked cheerfully. "Well, why don't you go to sleep? I know you can walk all night while we're on the road, but it's still good to sleep when you can enjoy an inn's nice clean bedding. Go ahead, get some rest."

"What about you?" I responded. "You always need to sleep more than I do. Admit you had a bad idea. At least you tried. There's no disgrace in that. Get some sleep, too, and in the morning we'll face Timothy together."

But Felix just insisted I go to sleep while he kept working, so I did, and despite my sincere concern about what would happen to us when Timothy found out we hadn't kept our bargain, I soon nodded off.

I woke in the morning to find Felix carving away, and sitting amid a huge pile of wood shavings. Nine completed planks were stacked beside him, and he was almost finished with the tenth. Each was beautifully decorated with carved images that looked real enough to jump off the surface of the wood.

"What kind of miracle is this?" I gasped, jumping up, tangling my feet in the bedding and falling flat on my face into the pile of wood shavings. I got some of the shavings in my mouth and had a coughing fit. Even as I coughed, I could hear Felix laughing.

"It's not a miracle, it's just some of our magic," he chuckled. "Maybe I should say it's my magic, something special to me. I just kept on carving, intending to stop when daylight came, and the more I carved, the longer it stayed nighttime. I'm not tired at all. I feel as if I could keep right on carving all day, but I won't because we have six days left and just one more plank to complete, not counting the one you've been working on. Do you think you'll be able to finish it in time for Timothy, or should I just include it with the other I'll carve tonight?"

Of course, we had all the covers ready for Timothy by the date upon which we'd agreed. He was excited to have them, and offered many loud compliments on the quality of the craftsmanship. Timothy had gotten his new six sets of gospels from the monks, and Felix and I helped him bind these to the covers we'd carved. Then all three of us carried the books to the marketplace and offered them for sale. The rich man in the blue robe was back, and he bought four gospels, paying an amazing amount of money for the privilege of owning them. The other two were quickly sold as well. Even after Timothy paid us, he still made a handsome profit. Everyone was happy.

Felix didn't stop there. He immediately agreed to carve Timothy a dozen more covers during the next week. Timothy had a friend who owned a ship; this friend took six finished sets of covers with him on his next voyage to Rome, and sold them in one of the marketplaces there. We soon fell into a pattern. Felix and I would travel around, giving our gifts in secret. Every few months when our money ran low, we'd buy wood planks and Felix would spend a few nights practicing his woodcarving magic. Then we'd contact Timothy, who would take the covers, sell them, and divide the profits with us. In this way Felix and I were able to make a comfortable living and keep on with our mission and travels. Timothy became our good friend. Eventually we revealed some of our secrets to him, and he worked even more closely with us.

Meanwhile, being the one to solve our money problem did Felix a great deal of good. He gained self-confidence from it and felt more assured that he would play an important part in whatever the future might hold for us. That certainly proved to be true.

We spent a few months in and around Constantinople, building up our new business with Timothy and planning further travels. In particular, the islands of Britain sounded interesting and we decided to see them for ourselves. Then, just a week before we planned to leave, Felix and I went out one night to give gifts to several needy children we'd seen. They were living in tents on the outskirts of the city. It turned out to be perhaps the most important night of my life.

The other person didn't cry out, but reached into another bag and withdrew
what appeared to be a thick club, waving it at me. We made silent,
threatening gestures: a pantomime of violence. For moments
it was frightening, then quickly turned absurd.

EIGHT

Layla

he first time I saw Layla, we were sneaking into the same tent. Earlier that day, Felix and I had noticed some ragged travelers in the Constantinople marketplace. They were trying to trade dirty blankets for food, but none of the merchants were interested.

When the travelers gave up and walked away, Felix and I followed them to the outskirts of the city, where they were camped in tents. Several hungry-looking children ran up to them as they approached, obviously hoping they'd returned with something to eat, but they hadn't. Felix and I nodded to each other. We returned to the marketplace and bought loaves of bread, large blocks of cheese, and lots of dried fruit. That night we loaded the food in our sacks and went back to the travelers' tents. No one sat around the smoking coals of the small campfire; everyone was obviously asleep.

We'd learned from long experience that Felix tended to trip and bump into things whenever he tried to be stealthy, so I took the sacks and cautiously approached the first tent. Although it was old and patched, it was still big, with several inside poles propping up the canvas and two entry flaps, one at each end. The tent had room for six or seven people. I peeked inside the nearest entry flap and saw the sleeping forms of two adults—mother and father, probably—and two children. Motioning for Felix to stay outside and keep watch, I quietly eased myself inside. Being careful not to disturb anyone, I moved to the side of the nearest sleeping child, a little boy who looked much too thin. Reaching into my sack, I took out a loaf of bread, a block of cheese, and some sun-dried dates. I put these by the foot of his sleeping mat. When he woke in the morning there'd be enough food for him and his whole family to enjoy a good breakfast. Then I moved to where the next child slept. I reached into my sack for another loaf, and as I did someone else came through the other tent flap and nearly bumped into me.

I'd come close to being caught before, many times. Some people had caught glimpses of me, but never had I come face-to-face with someone whose house or tent I'd entered uninvited, although I'd done so for a good purpose. Remember, these were lawless times. Intruders were assumed to have come to steal or murder. You attacked burglars before they could attack you. So, expecting to be assaulted, I waved my loaf of bread like a weapon, hoping to frighten the other person enough so an alarm wouldn't be raised before I could get out of the tent, find Felix, and run.

The other person didn't cry out, but reached into another bag and withdrew what appeared to be a thick club, waving it at me. We made silent, threatening gestures: a pantomime of violence. For moments it was frightening, then quickly turned absurd. Obviously the other person didn't want to be discovered, either. Well, if it was a thief, Felix and I could at least see nothing was stolen. I stopped waving the bread and gestured instead for the other person to follow me out of the tent.

Felix looked startled when he saw two people coming. I raised my index finger to my lips; everyone in the tents was still asleep. The three of us quietly moved to a few hundred yards away. Even when we stopped and began to whisper, I still didn't get a good look at the intruder, who wore a dark cloak with a heavy hood.

"Who are you, and what are you trying to do?" I whispered. "If you're a thief, leave these poor people alone. They don't have anything to steal."

"Speak for yourself!" came the whispered reply. "Did I interrupt your robbery? Well, if the two of you want to kill me, I'll give you a hard fight first!"

"Give us the weapon you have in your pack, and then we'll talk," I suggested, still whispering. Felix moved quietly beside the stranger and put his hand into the pack. He looked puzzled as he pulled out a loaf of bread just like the one I'd been waving.

"Wait a moment," he said, and reached in again. "There's only food in here. Bread, olives, and fruit."

"Go ahead and steal it," sneered the stranger, hissing and sounding disgusted. "Fill your own fat stomachs while those poor people starve, and I hope you get the bellyaches you deserve afterward."

"We're not stealing anything, and don't call me fat," I hissed back. "Do you mean to tell me you were going into the tent to leave food, not to rob that family?"

The stranger snatched the loaf back out of Felix's hand and put it back into the pouch. "I've never robbed anybody, which is more than I can say for you. Where's that club you threatened me with?"

"I don't have a club," I replied. "Here's what I was waving." I pulled out my loaf of bread. "It seems neither one of us is a robber. Well, I'd like to know you better, friend. My companion and I have a clean, warm room back in the city. Would you care to accompany us there? We could find something to drink and be comfortable."

"Perhaps, but first let's finish our errand," the stranger whispered, and I remembered why Felix and I had come to the camp in the first place. Happy to share an adventure with someone who obviously was kind, I agreed. The stranger left gifts in some tents, I did the same in others. When all our food had been quietly distributed, we rejoined Felix and returned to the city.

As we moved farther away from the tent camp, Felix and I began to talk in our normal voices. But the stranger never did, speaking seldom and then only in a whisper. When we arrived at the inn where Felix and I had our room, our invitation to come in for something to drink was refused with a simple shake of our new friend's head.

"What's wrong with you?" Felix asked. "You know we're not thieves. We're just two gift-givers who are pleased to meet another. Come on up; if you don't have a place to stay, you can even sleep here."

I thought this offer was generous, but the stranger didn't, whispering, "I have to leave. Good night." But I reached out, grabbed an arm, and said, "At least let me see who you are." I pulled back the stranger's hood and found myself looking into the face of a woman who was perhaps thirty-five years old.

"Let me go," she said firmly, no longer whispering but sounding very definite. "I can fight if I have to."

"Well, you don't have to," I said quickly. "Please, my good woman, don't be afraid we'd harm you. Really, we honor you. Our offer of something to drink is made in friendship."

The woman had huge dark eyes, the kind that look into other

people's hearts and instantly know all their secrets. She studied Felix and me carefully before saying, "Then in friendship I accept."

We sat in the room for hours drinking watered fruit juice—wine was too expensive; we preferred spending our money on things needed by others—and talking about ourselves. We learned her name was Layla, and that she came from a small village not too far from Patara, where I was born. Like me, Layla had been orphaned early in life. An aunt and uncle raised her. They were farmers who were lucky enough to have good harvests every year, and it was their pleasure to give all the extra food they had to those in need.

"As I grew up I began hearing stories about some mysterious man who, many years earlier, came secretly by night and left gifts by the sleeping mats of the poor," Layla explained. Felix looked amazed and poked me. I poked him back and muttered, "Be quiet."

"I always thought that was something I'd like to do, too," Layla continued. "When my aunt and uncle died, they left me their farm and a nice inheritance. Some of the men in my village thought they would marry me, but I knew it was because they wanted the farm and money and not because they loved me." She gestured at herself. "I'm not beautiful, after all."

Layla

"You seem beautiful to me," I said before I could stop myself, and, once the words were spoken, they seemed to hang in the air. Felix grinned like a fool. Layla blushed, and I swallowed hard. Soon afterward I asked where she was staying, and she named a place nearby that offered secure shelter to women traveling alone. "We'll escort you back," I suggested. "But will you please see us again tomorrow? I think we have a story to tell that might interest you."

She agreed. Felix and I walked back to her inn with her and waited while she knocked on the door. After she was safely inside, we turned to walk back to our own room.

"You like her, don't you?" Felix asked impudently.

"Of course I do," I replied carefully. "She gives gifts, just as we do."

"You like her for more than that," Felix teased. "She likes you, too. I think there's going to be a romance."

"There's going to be nothing of the kind!" I snapped. "Really, Felix, I'm more than one hundred thirty years old! That's too old to think about marriage."

"Well, you're the one speaking of marriage, or didn't you notice?" Felix pointed out.

"Don't talk to me," I mumbled, but when we were back in our room I dreamed the rest of the night about her beautiful eyes.

The next evening Layla joined us for supper. Later we distributed gifts to another poor family that had taken shelter in a rich man's barn. Layla insisted she buy her fair share of the cloaks and sandals we left behind as gifts. I could tell she was a woman of strong spirit and great self-confidence.

"If you like, we could go back to the inn and I could tell you a story you might enjoy," I suggested.

Layla agreed, and when we were seated and had fruit juice to drink, I began to tell her something of myself. It was strange to describe my early life again. Before, I'd only spoken of it to Felix. Layla listened carefully, her eyes peering into mine and apparently satisfying herself that I was telling the truth. I wasn't sure how much she should hear, but I ended up telling everything—about the first gifts to the daughters of Shem in Patara; my decision to become a priest; how people began to surround me all the time, and how I left Myra in the middle of the night to regain the privacy I needed for gift-giving; the way in which I first learned time and distance were different for me, and my meeting Felix in Rome. Finally, hesitantly, I told her how Felix and I had stopped aging. This last information was so outrageous, I worried Layla might laugh at me or call me a liar, but she didn't. My story took until dawn to tell, and when I finally finished, she sat quietly and looked at me with those wonderful eyes.

"So it was you all along," she said. "You did the deeds that inspired me. Well, how splendid."

"You believe me?" I asked hopefully.

She seemed surprised by the question. "Of course I do! No one could invent such an incredible tale. So now you and Felix will spend eternity doing good things for others—how blessed you are, how lucky!"

I couldn't help myself. "But it's lonely sometimes," I blurted. Felix, seated near me, looked rather insulted. I ignored him. "The task is so great. So many people need so much. And I need your help. Will you join me, I mean, join us?"

I propose marriage to Layla

"He's asking you to marry him, so I'm going to leave for a while," Felix interrupted, and bolted out the door before I could stop him.

"Are you?" Layla asked. "I'm not sure if you have or haven't."

I wanted to be angry with Felix, but I realized he'd only spoken the words I'd meant to say. "I suppose I am asking you to marry me," I admitted. "I've had no practice asking this before, so maybe I didn't do it properly. And it's all right if you say no."

"Of course I'll marry you, as long as you promise we can be equal partners in gift-giving," Layla said. "I can't imagine a happier life."

I wasn't certain what to do next. I thought about going to her and kissing her, but as I got to my feet another thought came to me.

"Layla," I asked. "What about how long you'll live? I mean, it seems Felix and I have stopped growing older, but what about you? I couldn't stand it if we married and I lived on and on, only to lose you along the way."

"Perhaps I'll be like Felix and stop aging, too," she suggested. "If I don't, well, who can tell the future, anyway?"

"I can't help but wonder—" I began, but she held up her hand for me to be quiet. What a strong-minded woman!

"Stop talking, Nicholas," she said firmly. "I think, since we're to be married, that you ought to come over here and kiss me instead."

So I kissed her, and a few days later we were married by the priest of a small church. He performed the wedding service in exchange for a set of Felix's finest carved-wood book covers. Then we moved on, Felix and Layla and me—three gift-givers ready for further adventures.

Attila leaned forward. "Tell me more," he begged, and I did. My whole
story flowed out of me, and my tale went back to the beginning
at Patara and all the way up to our capture by his scouts.

NINE

Travels with Attila

ecause there were always so many wars going on, it was hard to travel from one part of the world to another. Although the three of us somehow could travel faster than other humans, that advantage was only possible in countries at peace. Where there was danger from marauding armies, we had to make our way carefully, like everyone else.

Layla, Felix, and I had decided we should concentrate on exploring those countries where Christianity had spread, often by priests who'd ventured into the wilderness. These priests were usually allowed to travel unmolested. Christian armies gave them free passage and other armies knew priests had taken vows of poverty and didn't have anything worth stealing.

So the three of us did our best to move about quietly, avoiding battlefields and spending as much time as possible in villages. Whenever we were stopped and questioned, we said Felix and I were priests and Layla was a nun. We certainly looked poor, and took pains to hide the money we had with us. Most of our funds were left with Timothy, who would send messengers to us with more as we needed it.

Nighttime gift-giving continued; we all enjoyed it, especially Layla. Felix and I soon found how helpful it was to have a woman working with us. When we'd reach a village, Layla would mingle with other women in the marketplace or at the river washing clothes, and later she'd return knowing exactly what each child in the village needed.

But we also tried to learn as much as we could about each country we visited. We didn't know why this might someday be important. We only knew it was something we should do. All three of us were especially interested in the islands of Britain, which had long since become legendary in other parts of the world. Tales had it that the original Britons painted themselves blue and lived in trees. Later, the myths said, they were led by great wizards known as Druids. The Romans eventually made Britain part of their empire, but it was easier to claim the islands than to keep them. The Britons were wild warriors and resisted the Romans as well as any Roman foe had. Finally, the Romans decided to concentrate their forces closer to their homeland.

As soon as the Roman forces left, the Saxons saw their chance. These fierce fighters crossed the narrow channel between Europe and England in warships, always eager to give battle and never in the habit of being merciful to anyone weaker than they were. The Britons soon found themselves in desperate trouble.

Still, the first Christian priests had made their way to the islands, so Layla, Felix, and I decided to follow them there if we could. The year was 453 A.D., and by my best estimate I was one hundred seventy-three years old.

"I don't see how we're going to get across the water to those islands," Felix grumbled as we slowly made our way northwest. "And if we do get to Britain, what if we're the only ones there who haven't painted ourselves blue?"

"Then we'll paint ourselves blue, too," said Layla, who hadn't seemed to age a day since she'd married me forty-three years earlier. "Remember, we don't want to draw attention to ourselves."

"Too late for that," I interrupted. "We have unwanted company, and they've certainly noticed us."

We were in a forest near the Rhine River, and had heard from other travelers that the army of the great Hun chief Attila might be nearby. The Huns were a warlike people whose tribes originated in what is now called Germany. They'd been a constant problem for the Romans, and Attila had long been one of the most feared warriors in Europe. But in 451 A.D., the Romans had formed a temporary alliance with the Visigoths and together they'd defeated Attila in a day-long battle. He and his army fled, although everyone knew they'd be back again in force. As Felix, Layla, and I neared the Rhine, local rumor had it that Attila had returned, this time determined to invade Italy and conquer Rome itself.

The rumor was right. While Felix and Layla had been talking, I saw six Huns dressed in wolfskins and armed with bows and short spears emerge from behind nearby trees. They quickly surrounded us.

We'd spent much of our time learning different languages, so we were able to talk with them.

"Whose army do you fight with?" one of the Huns asked, pulling an arrow back on his bowstring and looking quite eager to shoot it at us.

Europe, as it would appear later

"No one's army," I answered as calmly as I could. "We're Christians trying to reach the islands of Britain. As you can see, we're very poor. But if you're hungry, we have bread and dried fruit in our packs. Would you like some?"

One of the warriors was very young, perhaps twelve. All six Huns were skinny, and this boy smiled when he heard me offer food. He started to move forward, but the first warrior, who seemed to be the leader, gestured for him to wait.

"You could be spies for the Romans," he said. "You look too fat to be a priest," he added, pointing at me. Layla giggled. "We'll take you to the leader and let him decide what to do with you."

The Hun camp was close by. We hadn't noticed it because Attila had ordered his men not to light many fires, thinking the smoke might give their presence away to the enemies. Our captors marched us up to the largest tent in the camp; it was made from stitched-together animal skins. When the leader came out, I knew he must be Attila. Though he was very short, his eyes were ice blue, and when he spoke it was obvious he was used to being obeyed.

"You say you're Christians on the way to Britain?" he asked harshly. "I don't believe it. The Romans sent you to spy on me."

"I don't think there are any Romans within a hundred miles," I said truthfully. "If there are, we haven't seen them, although you shouldn't take our word for it since we didn't see your army either. Look at how easily your men captured us. Could they have done this if we were really spies?"

Attila

Attila stuck a dirty finger in his mouth and began to pick his teeth with a long, cracked fingernail. Flies buzzed around him. I'm sorry to say he had a rather foul body odor.

"Well," he finally said, "I guess I have to either kill you or let you go. We've been marching fast and don't have any food to spare, so we can't keep you as prisoners."

"You really don't want to kill us," I said, trying to sound more confident than I felt. "We've done you no harm, and besides, aren't you tired of killing? Don't you often look at your sword and wish you never had to use it again?" I didn't know why I said this. The words just came hurrying out of my mouth.

Felix groaned, thinking I'd just said too much, and even Layla looked pale. Attila thought about killing us. I know I saw his fingers twitch near the hilt of his sword. But that tense moment passed. He looked at me thoughtfully and said, "Come into my tent. I guess I can feed one of you. The other two will stay out here. I won't waste guards on them. If they try to run, they'll regret it."

"Oh, we'll stay right here," Felix promised. Layla looked both relieved we hadn't been killed and angry that I was the only one invited into Attila's tent. She and Felix really didn't miss anything. It was dark in there, and smoke from the small fire hung in stinging clouds around our heads even after we seated ourselves on mats.

"How did you know I was tired of the killing?" Attila asked.

"Who wouldn't be tired of it?" I replied. "Hating wears a person down to nothing. Kindness is what brings true pleasure in life."

Attila leaned forward. "Tell me more," he begged, and I did. My whole story flowed out of me. My tale went back to the beginning at Patara, and all the way up to our capture by his scouts. Attila interrupted me once to call in one of his men and order food prepared for Felix and Layla, and that they be given a warm place to sleep. Then he and I talked until dawn, and when the sun rose there were four in our party, because Attila had decided to give up his life of war and join us.

"There's no sense in fighting, anyway," he admitted. "No matter how many battles we win, there is always another army ready to fight me. Oh, the Romans are weakening, but the Gauls are gaining strength, and the Franks and the Vandals prefer war to peace. I think I'll come with you to Britain and help you give your gifts there."

It didn't occur to Attila to ask if that was all right with me, and, anyway, it was. He was a scarred old warrior, but he had plenty of common sense. I knew he'd be especially useful in helping us locate and avoid other armies.

We left the next night. Attila picked a trusted captain to tell the rest of the Huns that their leader had died and would be buried in a secret place. They were to return to their homes and not fight any more if they could help it.

As a special favor, Attila asked if his wife could come, too. Dorothea turned out to be a very gentle woman who could sew beautifully, She soon patched all our ragged robes so well that they looked like new. Layla was worried Attila would get in fights with strangers we met—he never did, having fought as much as anyone could ever want already—but she was very pleased to have another woman to talk to. As for Felix, he developed a bad habit of teasing Attila, who would get angry and threaten him with terrible things, but never laid a hand on him.

So we were five when we finally reached the banks of the wide channel that separated our side of civilization from Britain. It was exciting to get that far, but we had no idea how to proceed.

"Maybe we could ask some Saxons for a ride on one of their warships," Felix suggested.

Attila fixed him with a fierce glare. "Saxons are terrible people," he snorted. "They'd rather kill someone like you, Felix, than give you a ride. Why don't you just throw yourself into this water and drown? If nothing else, that would give all our ears a rest."

Dorothea frowned at her husband. "Leave Felix alone. At least he's trying to think of something. Can we perhaps rent a small boat and sail across?"

"I considered that," I said, "but I don't think any of us are good enough sailors to handle a small boat. We'd be as likely to get swept away as we would be to land on the British shore."

As usual, Layla had the best suggestion. "Everything always happens to us for a reason," she said. "We're here because we're meant to be. So let's simply wait until someone comes to help us. There's time for a meal, and to rest our feet after this long journey. We have bread and cheese and a few olives. Who's hungry?" Of course, we all were, though Felix later accused me of eating more than my share.

After eating, we spread out our blankets and slept. I stayed awake longer than the others, although Layla kept me company for several hours before she finally fell asleep. I lay there in the darkness looking up at the stars, wondering how far away they were and what was going to happen to get all five of us across the water to Britain. My answer arrived with the first pink streaks of sunrise against the black night sky. There was the sound of water slapping against the prow of a boat, and sure enough a small vessel came into view, hugging the shoreline near us and piloted by a tall, slender man of middle age dressed in the rough brown robes of a priest.

"Come ashore and join us for breakfast," I called out to him, the sound of my voice waking the others. The priest in the boat waved and steered his craft to the shore in front of us.

"Christians?" he asked carefully, eyeing Attila with particular suspicion. Though we'd convinced Attila to exchange his animal furs for more common robes, and although he washed more regularly than he once had, the Hun chief still looked too fierce to be an ordinary missionary.

"We are," I said hurriedly. "This is my wife, Layla, and this is Felix, and these two fine people are Attila and his wife, Dorothea. They're from the Hun tribe."

The priest raised one eyebrow. "Attila" was hardly a common name. "Not too many Christians yet among the Huns," he said carefully.

"Let's eat," grunted Attila, who was never much for polite conversation. We got out more bread and some dried figs. The priest ate heartily, with the appetite of a man who'd missed many meals. I waited until he had satisfied his hunger before asking who he was and where he was going.

"My name is Patrick," he replied. "I spent much of my boyhood as a slave on an island far to the west of Britain. Ireland, it's called. I escaped from my captors and made my way to Rome, where I became a Christian priest. Since then I've often returned to Britain and Ireland. There aren't many priests there. Sometimes I'm given credit for doing miracles when I've really done nothing at all."

"Tell me about it," I urged, remembering all the miracles I was supposed to have worked in Myra, but hadn't.

"The story of the snakes is the most common," Patrick said. "A few years ago in Ireland, a village was infested with snakes, or so it was said. I'd never seen any there myself. But the people in the village told me that if I was really a priest I could make the snakes go away. Well, I raised my hands to the sky and cried, 'Snakes, be gone!' And none of the people in the village ever saw any snakes again, not that I believe they were around to be seen in the first place. Those people probably had looked in the grass and seen some crooked sticks. Still, it's rather handy to have a reputation for working miracles. I go around the country, identify myself, and people are usually willing to do whatever I ask, including not fighting with each other."

"We have hopes of seeing Britain, and from your story, I think we'd like to see Ireland, too," I suggested. "Perhaps you'd give us a ride across this wide channel of water in your boat. Do you have enough room?"

"I'm sure I do," Patrick said agreeably, "although I could only take such a large load for a short voyage to the other side. I mean no insult about your weight, friend," he hastily added, though not before Felix started guffawing. "Let me take you and your companions across to Britain, and if you ever get far enough west I'll try to find you on that coast and bring you the rest of the way to Ireland."

So we gathered our things, got in the boat, and were whisked across the channel to Britain. It wasn't an entirely calm passage. Poor Attila got seasick and made quite a mess at Felix's feet. He apologized to Patrick, who told the Hun chief not to worry about it. I noticed Attila didn't apologize to Felix, who made a point of washing his feet over and over when we'd safely disembarked on the British shore.

As soon as we saw the man, we knew he must be Arthur. There was a grandness about him, even as he lay in a bloody heap on the barn's dirt floor. With Attila's help, Dorothea raised him to a sitting position, and Layla got water from the old woman's tiny well.

TEN

Arthur of Britain

e found Britain to be a wild and beautiful country, with more lush forests and hills than any of us had ever seen. Although we'd arrived in early fall, the weather was still warm and delightful. In most ways, we felt we were in paradise.

But war was as much a part of Britain as the land's lovely green fields. Its native people were a primitive, proud race ready to fight foreign invaders for every inch of earth. When we got there, the Britons were involved in a long battle with Saxon war parties for control of the island's south and east regions. For forty years, the Saxons had been winning, never decisively but always ending each year by extending their control a few miles nearer to the fertile British midlands.

As usual, we spent our first few months in a new place exploring the countryside, visiting villages, and learning as much as possible about the new place and its customs. Above all, we soon learned that, along the southeast coast, life for ordinary British peasants was hard. Villages often were raided by the Saxons, who stole what they wanted, killed any men they could catch, and took away women and children as slaves. Villages spared from the Saxons fell prey to Britain's own war parties—which also needed food, at the expense of the countrymen they were trying to save from the invading enemy.

So there were plenty of families in need, and plenty of children who could use a nighttime gift of food or clothing. But for the first time we were in a place where such goods were hard to buy. We had a fair amount of money with us, coins small enough not to attract too much attention, but easily worth the purchase price of such things as we needed. We did the best we could. It was so rare for any charity to be shown on this island that right after our first few gift-givings, the story of the gifts began to circulate quickly from village to village.

Attila was quickest to fall in love with Britain. Although he'd wearied of participating in battles, he still was a student of warfare.

"The Saxons will eventually crush the Britons completely," he predicted, "but they'll pay for every inch of land with blood. These Britons are good fighters, ones who know when to stand and do battle and when to retreat."

Attila was especially impressed with a tribal war chief named Arthur. This fellow was a special torment to the Saxons, moving his small band of fighters quickly from one place to another and attacking where and when he was least expected.

"I think this Arthur must be interesting," Attila said. "Could we try to find him, Nicholas? I'd like to talk battle strategy with him. Perhaps I could give him some useful advice. I once outfought the Romans, you know."

"We'd best stay away from Arthur, because where he is, the fighting is likely to be the bloodiest," I replied. "Put warfare behind you, Attila. Our business is giving gifts, not giving battle."

Layla noticed the strained tone of my voice. That night when the others slept she quietly said to me, "Being near battles weakens your special powers, doesn't it? That's why we can move so quickly when no armies are nearby, and why we creep along close to battlefields. Attila's scouts would never have captured us if we'd been going at our usual speed, and now here in the south of Britain we don't seem able to get ourselves from village to village as quickly."

"In a way, I'm glad you noticed," I told her. "I'd hoped it was my imagination, but now I'm convinced of it. Where war is, we can't be, or at least we can't be as effective as we are in other places. What a waste war is! Look at this beautiful country, with plenty of room for everyone. But the Britons want to rule themselves or die, and these Saxons are driven to conquer rather than come in friendship. Will the world always be like this? Surely someday people will know better."

"Perhaps," Layla said doubtfully. "Why not get some rest if you can? Tomorrow we'll find a village, and in that village will be children in need, and tomorrow night we'll visit them with presents. Think about that, instead."

We spent the next year going from village to village, giving our gifts and trying our best not to be discouraged by the fighting all around us. Twice we were taken captive by Briton war parties, who'd mistaken us for Saxons, and once by Saxons who'd mistaken us for Britons. On all three occasions we were able to convince them otherwise. Luckily the Christian religion had, to an extent, reached both sides, for when we identified ourselves as missionaries we were quickly set free.

"Thank goodness these people have been converted," Felix said with relief after the Saxons let us go. "They're devout enough to send missionaries safely on their way."

"It's too bad they're not devout enough to remember the phrase 'Thou shalt not kill,' " I said sadly. "Yes, they let us live, but how many innocent people will die at their hands tomorrow?"

Twice during the year we sent messages to Timothy, who now was a very old man. His children ran his businesses for him. Along with our requests for money, we shipped him more wonderfully carved book covers and, for the first time, intricate wood figures shaped like soldiers. Attila had a knack for carving these, and Timothy was able to sell them in faraway marketplaces for almost as much as the book covers. We'd more or less told him our secrets as the years passed and we learned he could be trusted. He always gave us fair prices, and once we saw the lack of goods in England he began to pay us in shipments of wool cloaks and stout shoes. We stored these in barns of Briton farmers we befriended. A few times we lost barnfuls of goods to Saxon raiders, but for the most part we were lucky.

Food for gift-giving was much harder to come by. There was very little for sale, and what there was to buy was frankly horrible stuff—wormy meat and old, tough vegetables. Anything worth eating was gobbled up by whichever Britons were fortunate enough to get their mouths to it first. So there were no marketplaces full of food for sale like we'd been accustomed to frequenting in Constantinople, Rome, and other major cities during our travels.

Sometimes a few of us—Felix or me, most often—would complain out loud that we did little good in leaving shoes for a child who was in danger of starving. But Layla, sensible as always, offered a constant reminder: "What we're really giving these children is hope, and the knowledge that there are people in this world who care about

them. That's a gift even greater than food, so stop complaining."
And we'd stop.

Although we were across the channel from Europe, word of
events there would often reach us. The most important news was
that the Romans had been driven from Gaul, the country that later
would be called France. Clovis, the war chief of the Franks, not only
defeated the Romans but the Visigoths, too. It seemed he might be
the powerful leader who could eventually bring peace to the land,
even if he had to accomplish this by killing off everyone else. I felt
somewhat better when I learned that he chose Christmas Day 496
A.D. to be baptized, along with thousands of his followers. The
Christian Church was delighted, of course, and Clovis proved himself to be more than a mere warrior by spending much of the rest of
his life inventing laws to govern daily conduct.

There was no such clear-cut leader on the island of Britain. The
Saxons continued their bloody invasion and the Britons persisted in
defending themselves. Arthur became the unofficial leader of the
Britons, who were divided into too many squabbling tribes to put up
a united defense against the Saxons. Arthur tried to talk other tribal
chieftains into joining together, and for a while it appeared he might
be successful. In the year 500 A.D., Arthur even led a number of
tribes against the Saxons in Dorset, a region of southeast Britain,
and beat the invaders back toward the sea. Bards or storytellers of
the Celtic tribes began traveling around singing songs and telling
stories about the great and bold Arthur, the war chief who'd saved
the Britons, but they sang too soon. The Saxons returned more
determined than ever to conquer the island, and Arthur's tribal alliance was smashed apart by the invaders' new attacks.

It became clear with Arthur's defeat that the Saxons would now

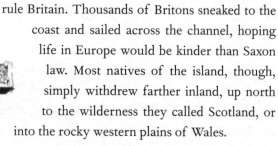

The Celtic Cross
of Ireland

rule Britain. Thousands of Britons sneaked to the coast and sailed across the channel, hoping life in Europe would be kinder than Saxon law. Most natives of the island, though, simply withdrew farther inland, up north to the wilderness they called Scotland, or into the rocky western plains of Wales.

Our group chose to stay close to the southeast coast. Most of the fighting was over. There were rumors that Arthur had been killed, perhaps stabbed in the back by one of his own captains who'd betrayed him to the Saxons. More hopeful Britons whispered that perhaps Arthur had only been badly wounded, and would come back in all his warrior glory someday to free their island of foreign rule.

The truth was, Arthur had been wounded, though not fatally. We knew this because a few days after he lost a final battle to the Saxons, an old woman cautiously approached us as we were walking by a small farm in the countryside a few miles from the battle site.

"Pardon, strangers, but are you some of those Christians?" she asked. I noticed the poor woman was wearing rags, and most of her teeth were missing. She went on, "If you are, and if you give help to others like they say Christians do, could you come see a wounded man? He's badly hurt, and I don't know what to do for him."

Dorothea had a great deal of experience assisting wounded men, having spent most of her marriage following Attila from battle to battle. She and Layla hurried ahead to the barn where the old woman said the wounded man lay unconscious. Felix, Attila, and I followed.

As soon as we saw the man, we knew he must be Arthur. There was a grandness about him, even as he lay in a bloody heap on the barn's dirt floor. With Attila's help, Dorothea raised him to a sitting position, and Layla got water from the old woman's tiny well. Dorothea bathed the wounded man's face. He had two deep cuts across his midsection and a nasty gash across his forehead. As Dorothea cleaned his face, his eyes fluttered open.

"Who are you?" he whispered, his legs jerking convulsively as he tried to get to his feet.

"Sit back, Arthur," Attila ordered in the softest tones I'd ever heard him speak. "Rest, brave chief. Your battle is done for a while, and the time to heal has begun."

"How do you know who I am?" Arthur wanted to know.

"One warrior knows another," Attila said briefly, and then told Felix, Layla, and me to wait outside while he and Dorothea inspected Arthur's wounds. The three of us left the barn and joined the old woman, who was fearful any Saxons hunting for Arthur would burn her farm if they found him there.

"It's him; it's the great Arthur, isn't it?" she asked, and we told her it was. "Well, he's got to leave right away. I came out to get eggs from my chickens and there he was in the barn, looking like he must have crawled in there during the night. I feel sorry for him, but I can't hide him here, don't you see? My husband's away hunting, and we're too old to start over if the Saxons find that man here and burn us out because of it."

Dorothea

Layla looked at me, the question reflected in our eyes. When I nodded, she said, "Don't worry. Let our friends tend to the man's wounds, and then we'll take him with us."

Arthur

And that is what happened. Arthur was very weak, so for the first two days Attila fashioned a sort of stretcher with strong cloaks tied between a pair of long, trimmed tree branches. He, Felix, and I took turns two at a time carrying the stretcher with Arthur on it. His wounds healed quicker than his mind, which retained memories of what had to have been a terrible battle. At night Arthur would toss and moan, no doubt dreaming of Saxon warships and cruel invaders arriving on them.

On the third day he was able to walk part of the time. We were moving west. Attila thought the Saxons would be so proud of their victory that they'd stay near the coast to celebrate for a while. As we got farther from the battlefields, we were able to travel faster. I thought we might as well go all the way to Ireland and visit Patrick.

That night Attila drew Arthur aside and spent hours talking with him quietly. I could only guess, but I thought he might be telling Arthur about his own victories and defeats and how he'd eventually decided even the bravest warrior could only fight for so long. Apparently his words touched Arthur. The next day our newest companion walked along with the rest of us, despite having little to offer in the way of conversation. That took longer, but in another week when we'd reached the far west coast and gotten passage on a small ship to Ireland, Arthur had started entertaining us with stories of British history. He was a very good storyteller, far better than the rest of us, and a talented hand with a carving knife. Between Felix, Attila, and Arthur, we had three men who could turn bits of wood into almost anything imaginable.

It wasn't hard to find Patrick, who had become the most famous man in Ireland. His followers had built him a fine stone church, with a sturdy log hut covered with a thatched roof beside it so the good missionary would have a dry place to sleep. We sent word ahead to Patrick of our impending arrival, and when we arrived he welcomed us with a meal. He might have driven snakes out of Ireland, but he'd kept the rabbits. Two fine fat ones were roasting over Patrick's fire.

"I knew you and Felix would be hungry." He grinned. "After our meal, I'll want to hear about everything that's happened to you, and how you gained another companion. But take your time as you talk. All there ever seems to be in this world anymore is war and killing, so let's enjoy fellowship and peace here for a little while before we go out into the confusion again."

Charlemagne was a tall man with a long gray beard. He had something of
the look of a warrior, standing straight and staring at me with an expression
of curiosity, not fear. But there was great wisdom in his face, too.

ELEVEN

The Dark Ages

ot much really worth telling about happened during the next six centuries. When scholars are feeling generous, they refer to this period as "The Middle Ages," but its most common—and correct—nickname is "The Dark Ages." Almost everyone living in Europe and Britain spent these hundreds of years in misery. Wars were fought everywhere. Different tribes battled each other for control of bits and pieces of land. Warriors did what they wanted and common people suffered for it. No one was safe from the sword.

The six of us—Attila, Dorothea, Arthur, Felix, Layla, and I—spent these centuries doing what good we could. Often, we couldn't do much. Our travel was slow; as I'd learned previously, being anywhere near fighting reduced our ability to travel at wondrous speeds, and there always seemed to be fighting wherever we went. Timothy's

heirs continued to accept our carved book covers and whittled figures, and sell them for us, but their ships were frequently attacked by
pirates. We had less money to spend and often there was nothing
worthwhile to buy with the money we had. What a sad, terrible time!

Yet, while Europe wallowed in despair, other parts of the world
flourished. In 570 A.D., a man named Muhammad was born in the
Arab city of Mecca. By the time of his death in 632 A.D., he'd sown
the seeds of a new religion, Islam. In 589 A.D., China, a nation we'd
heard of only in the vaguest terms, was united under one ruler for
the first time in four centuries. Four years later, an island nation
eventually known as Japan developed its first central government
and laws.

Europe remained, for the most part, primitive. Brave missionaries gradually won most of the tribes over to Christianity, but this
new religion seemed to have little effect on all the fighting. Stories
about Jesus and his life were often intermingled with more supersti-
tious tales. Legends sprouted everywhere. In some places, it was still
believed dragons might be lurking.

People whose everyday lives are desperate often look to myths
for comfort. In these years, the people of Europe wanted miracles to
happen to them, so they easily accepted outrageous tales of miracles
involving others. Our small, six-member band knew all about this,
and we should have, because many of the made-up stories involved
Attila or Arthur or me.

Attila, who'd simply left his army to join us, now was widely
reported to have died in a fit of bad temper, then buried in a secret
place made even more secret by his captains deliberately killing
everyone associated with the burial. The rest of us knew from his
own stories that Attila had been, in his time, a rather cruel fighter,

but even he was amazed to hear stories of how he had preferred drinking his wine from human skulls.

"I suppose I might have done that if I'd thought of it," Attila said with a wry grin. "I must have shrunk, too. I heard recently that I was seven feet tall."

Still, tales of Attila were nothing compared to legends involving Arthur. As the years passed into decades, then centuries, it became widely believed in Britain that this simple war chief had actually been a king with a crown, one who lived with hundreds of fine knights and ladies in a magical castle called Camelot. Poems were written about Arthur; songs were composed and sung about him. At first, native Britons told these stories to give themselves hope that the hated Saxons would someday be driven back to Europe; but when the Normans crossed the channel in their turn and conquered the Saxons, the Arthur stories continued. Now, the stories went, he was being kept in some wonderful cave, asleep in the company of a magician named Merlin. Both would reappear soon, whenever "soon" might be.

And I, too, became the subject of more myths. Many of these stemmed from a new church policy of recognizing a select few men and women after their deaths as saints—people who were especially touched by God and who performed miracles during their lives. After saints had passed away, they were still supposed to be able to help those who prayed to them for assistance.

I was named a saint. Now memories of Nicholas, Bishop of Myra, became memories of Saint Nicholas, the man who in life was able to do wondrous things such as guide sinking ships safely into harbor and rescue children from all kinds of harm. In return for these acts, I was now considered patron saint of sailors and children, an embarrassing honor since I hadn't done any of it.

"If it's any comfort, I don't think I ever lived in the fabulous castle called Camelot," Arthur said jokingly. Often at night we'd entertain ourselves by reciting the latest myths we'd heard that involved each of us. "Nicholas, I once thought it was magic enough that I've joined you and lived to be—what?—three hundred years old already. But that's a little thing compared to living in enchanted castles and being named king of a whole country. I don't think the real magic would be splendid enough for the people who make up stories about us."

"Don't make fun of those who tell or believe the stories," Layla cautioned. "Many people have no joy in their own lives, so they let their imaginations work freely. Let's talk about other things, like the coronation of Charlemagne. Could he be the leader who will finally make things better?"

She said this just after December 25 in 800 A.D. Charlemagne, king of the Franks, had chosen that Christmas Day in Rome to be crowned emperor of the West by Pope Leo III. He picked the date because it was already a time of special celebration for Christians.

All over Europe and Britain, new ceremonies had gradually been added to the traditional Christian festivities on Christmas. In 529 A.D., Roman Emperor Justinian had declared December 25 a civic holiday on which none of his subjects could work. This news pleased me greatly. Most people had to labor too hard for their meager wages.

As Christian missionaries traveled throughout the world, they began to take winter customs of various nations and combine them with Christmas worship. In northern Europe and Britain, for instance, native peoples had long since had their own celebrations in December, mostly for the winter solstice. To symbolize their faith during snowy winter months that warm planting weather would eventually come again, they hung out evergreen branches in front of their homes.

"Julmond," as these people called it, also required feasting afterward as another mark of confidence that times of plenty would return.

The Christian missionaries, seeing all this, carried tales back to central Europe of "Jul," pronouncing the "J" like a "Y." Soon enough, proper Christians began hanging out evergreen branches as part of their celebration of Christ's birth. A similarly named custom came to central Europe from Persia, where end-of-the-year customs included burning part of a log in the season called "Yole," the fire being an offering along with prayers for good weather during the next planting season. "Jul" and "Yole" eventually became "Yule," another name for the Christmas season that continues to be used to this day.

Amid all the other bad times, people began to consider the Christmas holiday a very special, happy occasion. For one day, at least, fighting was usually forgotten. Charlemagne's choice of Christmas for his coronation was the clearest sign yet that even the greatest war leaders recognized the significance ordinary people placed on December 25.

By this time, we were in the western Frankish region of Burgundy, now part of France, at the time of Charlemagne's crowning, news of which had been carried across the continent by messengers. After so many centuries of discouragement, we wanted to meet this new emperor whose rule promised to be special. Charlemagne was supposed to be spending the rest of the winter camped outside Rome—he had little use for the fancy palaces in the city—so we set off, traveling east and south until we crossed into Italy.

Ever practical, Layla wanted to know what I'd say to Charlemagne. "Will you tell him everything about us, and ask him to leave his army and come with us like Attila and Arthur?" she wondered.

"Charlemagne has his own important mission, so I'd be wrong to

Western Frankish area of Burgundy

ask him to abandon it to join in ours," I replied. "I just want to meet the man so I can see with my own eyes that there's reason to hope for better times."

"It's probably going to be hard to see him," Felix predicted. "They say he's trying to do everything at once: build a government, start schools, and encourage artists to paint and write. Hundreds of important people every day are surely begging for an hour of his time. He'll hardly be interested in talking to strangers."

Felix was right; when we arrived in Charlemagne's camp and asked to see him, we were told the new emperor was much too busy. We left, spent a week giving gifts at night to poor children in the many villages surrounding Rome, then went back and asked again. The answer was the same.

"That's enough," said Attila, who was never especially patient.

"This emperor has no time for us, so let's go back to the countryside somewhere and do our gift-giving as best we can."

"Let's go back to Britain," Arthur said hopefully. "We haven't been there in a hundred years. I'd like to see the green hills again, and give gifts to all the needy children who live in them."

"We will, we will," I said, being careful not to promise anything specific. "Tonight, when the rest of you are out leaving gifts, I'll stay at our campsite and think about this." But as soon as they were gone I put on my red bishop's robes—not the original ones, which long since had been worn out, but newer ones sewn by Dorothea— and crept into Charlemagne's camp. The emperor was living in a big tent. I hid myself in some bushes until Charlemagne sent away all of his staff for the night. Then I quickly, quietly ducked inside.

Charlemagne was a tall man with a long gray beard. He had something of the look of a warrior, standing straight and staring at me with an expression of curiosity, not fear. But there was great wisdom in his face, too.

He greeted me by saying, "I don't think you've come to try and kill me. I see both your hands, and neither is holding a weapon. Your robes are those of a priest, and I'm a good friend of the church, so you can't be angry about that. Why are you here?"

"I just wanted to talk to you, Emperor," I answered. "For a week, one of your staff has said you were too busy. So I thought I'd wait until you were alone and might have time for a conversation with a stranger."

Charlemagne raised his eyebrows a little; he wasn't used to being spoken to so plainly. Then he nodded, smiled, and said, "Well, then, here you are. Would you like something to drink or to eat? No? Well, here's a bench. Sit down and we'll talk."

And we did. I asked Charlemagne how he planned to use his new powers as emperor, and he told me of his plans for a united Europe that offered protection to people who needed it, with free trade between countries and free education so children could learn enough to earn good livings when they grew to be adults.

"I never learned to read very well, and I can't write at all," he admitted. "I was lucky enough to be born in a royal family, but if I'd been born to a poor man and woman I'd only have been considered fit for herding sheep. The more education people have, the less they'll fight, because they'll be smart enough to find other ways to solve their problems. Now, what about you? There's something about you that makes me think you're a fellow with many secrets, and that you're someone who's seen a lot of this world."

I didn't tell him everything. I just said some companions and I traveled about finding children in need and helping them with gifts. Charlemagne asked where we got money to buy these gifts and I told him how we carved book covers and figures.

"Don't you have any rich friends who will give money to buy the gifts that you leave?" he asked, and when I said we didn't, he got out parchment and a goose-quill pen. "Can you write? Well, then, write down what I'm about to tell you, which is an order to all my captains and officers to bring you into my presence whenever you like, and to give you food and other supplies for your party whenever you need them. I can't give you money. What I have comes from taxes and every coin is needed for the programs I'm starting. But at least getting more traveling supplies for free will let you use all the money you make to buy those gifts you give to poor children."

Charlemagne dictated a lengthy order. When I'd written everything down he heated wax and put a blob of it on the parchment. Then he took a heavy metal disk, his official seal, and stamped it on the wax. This seal meant that the emperor himself had given the written order to assist "Nicholas and any of his trusted friends, these being named Layla, Arthur, Felix, Dorothea, and Attila."

"Attila," Charlemagne muttered. "An unusual name, isn't it? The only person I've heard of called Attila was a fierce old Hun chief who—well, I suppose it doesn't matter. That other Attila was eight feet tall and drank wine from a human skull, you know."

"Really?" I said politely. "No, that's not my Attila at all. The Attila who travels with me is of normal height, and he uses a simple cup."

Charlemagne laughed. "Well, the man I'm thinking of had to have died a long time ago, anyway. If he were living today, he'd have to be three hundred or three hundred fifty years old. Impossible!"

"Right," I agreed, thinking to myself that Attila was really closer to four hundred. "Well, thank you for your time and your gift, great Emperor. We'll remember you in our prayers, and many more children will have warm clothing or food to eat because of your kindness."

"Do me one favor, Nicholas," Charlemagne said as I pulled up a flap and prepared to leave his tent. "Always keep December twenty-fifth special. It works wonders on human hearts, and I think more good is accomplished on that day than is done all the rest of the year. I don't know why I wanted so badly to tell you that, but now I have, and I feel very peaceful. Visit me again whenever you like. Just show that order to my guards."

I visited Charlemagne on several occasions before he died fourteen years later. He continued to be a good and just ruler. Not all of Charlemagne's fine plans worked. His son Louis succeeded him as emperor of the West; he died in 840. After Louis, Charlemagne's successors weren't quite as powerful. But they did rule what became known as the Holy Roman Empire, which existed from 962 until 1806.

And when people told stories of Charlemagne, they often mentioned his determination that children should grow up in peace, and be well educated. So that idea survived, and remained a beacon of hope as Europe stumbled through several more unenlightened centuries.

Layla, who'd been breaking up small branches and adding them to
the fire, poked a stick into the flames so sharply that sparks crackled
and jumped. We all had to slap our blankets to make
sure they wouldn't start smoldering.

TWELVE

"Let's Give Gifts
of Toys!"

ne night about three hundred fifty years after Charlemagne died, Felix, Attila, Dorothea, Arthur, Layla, and I were sitting around the campfire in the hills of southeast Britain. It was a large fire, because autumn had arrived and the night air was cool. We'd eaten dinner—bread, fruit, cheese; nothing fancy, but still good, filling food—and now we were all lounging on our blankets.

Our conversation stuck to ordinary subjects, such as how much money we had left with which to buy gifts, and when we ought to take a long trip southeast to Rome (where officials of the Holy Roman Empire still honored Charlemagne's order to give us all the traveling supplies we required). The parchment on which that original order was written had long since crumbled with age. We'd requested a replacement copy, and gotten it, then needed a replacement for the replacement, and a replacement for that replacement, and so on. None of the officials we spoke to seemed to notice we didn't age along with the parchment. They just gave us what we wanted without paying much attention.

"I think we should spend the whole next century in Rome," Felix said thoughtfully. "In this last century, Britain's been more of a battlefield than ever. You had the Saxons being conquered by the Normans, and the Danish wanting to invade, and the wild tribes up in Scotland threatening to come south. Anywhere else would have been more peaceful."

"Think again," Arthur said, sounding irritated. He always took it personally whenever Britain was criticized for anything. "Italy's just a stopping-over place for all those knights going on the Crusades. We'd see more swords and armor there than we would if we stayed here."

I sighed unhappily, because it was true. The worst of the latest wars found Christian soldiers from Britain and Europe uniting in armies to attack the Muslims, who'd taken control of the ancient lands of the Jews, including the holy city of Jerusalem. Instead of asking for permission to share the city, the Christians decided to fight for it. Sometimes they fought better than others; in the so-called First Crusade of 1095 they'd actually recaptured Jerusalem, but the Muslim leader Saladin soon won it back.

A recent crusade, led by kings Philip II of France and Richard I of England, had been a miserable failure. Richard, who was called the Lion-Hearted by his subjects, had been captured by the Duke of Austria on his way back home. The duke was asking for a large ransom. Richard's brother John, who'd been left in charge of Britain while the king was away fighting, didn't seem in any hurry to raise the money. No one in England knew what might happen next. Civil war, matching those lords and knights loyal to John against those remaining loyal to Richard, seemed to be coming.

"Well, what will we do then, Nicholas?" Attila asked. "When I was a younger man, say, perhaps two hundred years old, I might have thought people would sooner or later get tired of fighting. But with the wisdom of very advanced years, I have to say I'm not certain they ever will. We've been hoping for centuries that better times might be coming. Maybe they're not."

Layla, who'd been breaking up small branches and adding them to the fire, poked a stick into the flames so sharply that sparks crackled and jumped. We all had to slap our blankets to make sure they wouldn't start smoldering.

"You have no right to be discouraged, Attila," she said sternly. "Our long lives are all the proof we need that things will get better someday, and I think they'll get better a lot faster if we don't spend so much time moping."

Attila looked hurt. Tough old warrior that he was, he still had very delicate feelings. Dorothea reached over and patted him gently on the leg, saying quietly but firmly, "Attila wasn't moping. He was just saying what's been on all our minds, Layla. How many thousands of nights have we gone out and left food and clothing for poor children, and what difference has it really made? The wars continue; poverty is everywhere. There's no way to be sure we're really making a difference. Nicholas, you're our leader. Do you know something the rest of us don't, some secret you could share so we'd feel more hopeful?"

I shrugged. "Things keep changing for the worse. Sooner or later they'll have to change for the better. There are so many new nations now: Denmark, Norway, Germany, Iceland, Poland—maybe their armies will be satisfied with what they have and stop fighting."

"Don't forget rumors of a New World," suggested Arthur. In recent decades he'd become fascinated with tales about boats sailing west and not falling off the edge of the world, but instead discovering new lands, countries rich beyond belief with forests full of wild game. As early as 875, Irish sailors were said to have done this, although the Irish kept few accurate records. But it was almost certain that in 982 Eric the Red, son of a Norwegian chieftain, sailed to some far-off country after being banished from Iceland for murder; he called this new place Greenland for its color. In 1001, Eric's son—appropriately named Lief Eric's Son, or Ericson—followed his father's example by sailing west as well and discovering a place he named "Vinland" because he found grape vines growing there.

Sometimes Arthur suggested we take passage on one of these expeditions and see these wonderful places for ourselves. But the rest of us remembered how Attila often got seasick and wouldn't agree to such a long, turbulent voyage.

"Rather than speculate about a New World, I think we should talk about what we're doing in this old one," I suggested. "Does anyone else share this feeling I've had for quite some time that there must be a better way to do what we do? I mean, we all work hard to see poor children get food and clothing, but the comfort these bring is only temporary. Food gets eaten, and children soon outgrow clothing. Since we move about so much and try to give to as many different children as we can, the ones we feed and clothe one night will be hungry again the next night, and ragged again the next month. What real good are we accomplishing?"

I half hoped my longtime companions would all rise up and begin shouting that I was wrong, that my words mocked the great things we'd done. Instead, they responded with nods and murmurs of agreement.

It was no surprise that Layla, always outspoken, was first to reply at length.

"I've been wondering when you'd come to this conclusion, Nicholas," she said. "As much as I've loved the idea of helping you help others, for decades, maybe even centuries, I've had the same doubts. There's nothing wrong with our intentions, but perhaps we haven't thought enough about the way in which we carry them out. Food nourishes the body, and clothes keep the body warm and dry. But it's the spirit inside the body that's most important. I think we've neglected the spirit."

Felix spoke next. Though he'd never said so, I often guessed he felt he should be second-in-command because he'd been with me longest, longer even than Layla. "I want to say we've postponed this discussion too long, but it wastes time to think of what we might have done differently in the past," Felix commented, looking first at the fire, then at each of us in turn. "The right question is, what should we do in the future? It's not just the gifts we've been giving, either, but the way in which we acquire them. The carved wooden book covers are bringing less and less income. Books aren't that rare anymore, and more craftsmen are turning out covers the way trees turn out leaves. We need to find a different way of making money."

Attila said impatiently, "Let's think about money after we've decided how we want to spend it. Nicholas, if we're not going to give food or clothing, what should we give?"

"Toys." Dorothea, usually the quietest among us, spoke this one word and the rest of us fell silent. We were all thinking.

"Toys," Layla repeated. "There may be something to that."

We hadn't discussed this subject much before. In that year of 1194, toys weren't something every child owned. They weren't even common. Babies sometimes were given rattles—hollow gourds with pebbles inside. Marbles were made of river clay. There were occasional balls of cloth that could be thrown back and forth. Hoops and tops were rare, prized possessions. And at county fairs and bazaars, puppet shows had become instantly popular with adults and children alike. But the fact of the matter was that simply surviving occupied everyone's attention most of the time. Anything beyond the most necessary elements of life—food, shelter, clothing—had to be an afterthought. The money to buy toys, or the time to make them, were luxuries far beyond the means of most families. So children usually had no toys at all.

Adults had a few games. Chess was first played in India in about 500 A.D. The Persians learned the game there, and a few centuries later introduced it to Europeans. And it was about 500 A.D. that dolls made of cloth were found in Egypt. The Egyptians were clever craftsmen; they also gave their children carved wooden crocodiles with jaws that opened and closed.

There were no wooden crocodiles, though, in the European countries where we spent most of our time. Until Dorothea's comment, I think it's fair to say none of us had ever really thought much about toys at all. But now that she had mentioned them, it was easy to remember the way children's faces lit up on those rare occasions when they had wooden tops to spin or cloth dolls to play with.

"As you said, food gets eaten immediately and clothes wear out quickly," Felix mused. "But if we could give children toys so they could play—"

"Then the joy from the toys might last much, much longer!" Arthur interrupted excitedly. "Nicholas! Let's give gifts of toys!"

Sometimes new ideas, ones never considered before, are obviously perfect. This one was. We spent the rest of that night and the next several weeks camped there in England, not arguing about *whether* we should give toys, but rather deciding *how* we should give them.

The first and most obvious problem was how to get enough toys to give. No big companies were manufacturing toys, and there weren't any toy stores where we could buy them. To make them ourselves, we'd have to purchase large amounts of raw materials— wood, cloth, and so forth. The magic would probably allow the six of us to carve, sew, and otherwise build toys faster than any hundred other craftsmen could, but we still couldn't make enough each day to deliver them every night as gifts to all the children whose hard lives would be made happier by receiving them.

"Well, then, why don't we spend three weeks of every month making toys, and one week of the month delivering them?" Attila asked. All of us found this suggestion agreeable.

Felix added, "And, little by little, why don't we change the goods we make and sell from wooden book covers to toys?

Failed, early attempts at making toys

Rich parents would buy them for their children, and the money they give us for them will pay for the toys we give poor children. Doesn't that seem appropriate?"

"It does," I said enthusiastically. "Dorothea, we have you to thank for this." Dorothea, a modest woman, blushed. Attila gave her an enthusiastic hug.

"That's my wife," he boasted. "She should have been the war chief. Then we Huns would have won every battle!"

We spent the next few dozen years making a modest beginning. Our first toys were complete failures. We didn't make marbles from the right clay, so our first ones simply broke in pieces when they smacked into each other. None of us knew how to cure wood strips with water to make perfectly circular hoops. The egg-shaped ones Attila and Arthur made rolled in crazy directions. Even Dorothea's and Layla's puppets and dolls looked more like mittens, until they learned how to sew them better.

But we experimented until we got everything right, and when we did we took several sacks of samples to a fair in Rome, where every toy we had was sold within an hour. We used the profits to buy materials for more toys. These we distributed by night as gifts to poor children. How heartwarming it was to return the next morning and find them shrieking with delight as they rolled hoops, shot marbles, or played at make-believe puppet shows.

"I know they're still dressed in rags, and that most of them will be hungry when they go to sleep tonight," Layla said. "But at least they're happy today, and tomorrow they'll have their toys to play with again."

Two years passed; Francis's idea of a nativity scene to help celebrate
December 25 spread quickly. A few villages had great debates about
whether it was really proper to act out the night of Jesus' birth since the
actors would be mere humans, while Jesus, Mary, and Joseph were holy.

THIRTEEN

The Man Who
Changed Christmas

he man who changed Christmas forever wasn't always known as Saint Francis of Assisi. In 1182, a wealthy Italian merchant and his wife named their newborn son Giovanni Bernardone. Young Giovanni was twelve in the year Dorothea suggested we give toys for presents instead of food and clothing.

Unfortunately, Giovanni was quite spoiled as a youth. His family was rich; their home was one of the grandest anywhere in Italy. Giovanni had more clothes than he could wear, more food than he could eat, and, I'm sure, every kind of toy that had so far been invented. Giovanni's father expected his oldest son to gradually take over the family business, and this is exactly what Giovanni did.

But in those days, no city completely escaped war, and it was common for powerful Italian "city-states" to battle each other. When Giovanni was nineteen, Assisi got into a squabble with Perugia. As a member of one of Assisi's most prominent families, Giovanni was expected to help lead the fighting. Well, he ended up being captured instead. The Perugians tossed him into prison, and he had been in there for over a year by the time the war ended in 1203.

Giovanni was different when he got out of prison. He had spent most of his time in a cell thinking about the world and his responsibilities in it. He changed his name to Francis in 1205, the same year he told his father he no longer wanted to be a rich merchant. The name change was important—people who wanted to give up worldly things for a life of religion often did this. A different name showed that they were different, too.

The newly named Francis began living a life that was exactly the opposite of his pampered childhood. He gave up everything he owned and walked around in ragged robes. Any money given to him was immediately used to buy food for the poor. It seemed to Francis that many Christian leaders only told people about how they'd be punished if they didn't do what God wanted, instead of concentrating on how all Christians should be friends and help each other. Four years after he'd left his father's house, Francis started a new program for others—priests, monks, and laypeople—who felt the same way. In Francis's honor, they called themselves "Franciscans," and dedicated themselves to doing good things for people. This group is still around today, so obviously Francis had the right idea.

Francis wasn't afraid of traveling long distances to spread his message. In 1212 he tried to go to Syria with the plan of converting Muslims to Christianity, or, failing that, to at least convince them that Muslims and Christians shouldn't fight anymore. Francis never got there. His ship was wrecked on the coast of Croatia, and he had to return to Europe. Another attempted trip to Morocco didn't work out, either. Poor Francis got sick in Spain and once again had to turn back. He was very discouraged.

But no hero gives up, and Francis of Assisi was a real hero. In 1219 he finally managed to get to an intended destination—Egypt, where he spent a month with that country's leaders talking about Christianity and how we should all be kind to each other. The Egyptian leaders didn't become Christian, but they began treating their people better.

When Francis got back to Italy after that trip, he decided to concentrate on problems in his native country. Too many uneducated people didn't really understand what they heard about the church, he concluded, and so he left his small group to travel around by himself. Francis would go to tiny villages where most people couldn't read or write, and he'd sing the gospel passages, which is how priests usually conducted a part of their church services. But instead of singing in Latin, the official language of the church, he'd sing in Italian so everyone could understand the words. This thoughtfulness made ordinary people love Francis very much. Since he insisted on remaining poor himself, the villagers would often invite him to live in their small homes for a while, and to join them when they celebrated different holidays, including Christ's birthday.

And it was in a small Italian village on December 24, 1223, that the rest of us met Francis. Layla, Felix, Arthur, Attila, Dorothea, and I had been traveling nearby, visiting small farming communities for a few nights to learn which children lived there, and then using one last night to enter their homes and leave them toys. We didn't have to wonder which children might be poor; all of them in that area were. We did some night gift-giving on December 23, then found ourselves the next morning in a village where Francis also happened to be. It was a tiny place; Francis was standing in its square singing some gospels in Italian to about twenty people, and when we heard his high, melodic voice we stopped to listen, too.

After Francis was finished singing, he thanked everyone for listening. He said a short prayer, then prepared to walk to the next village and do the same thing again. Francis was a short, thin man dressed in very shabby robes. He looked tired and thirsty, so we offered him a drink from the water gourds we carried.

"Thank you," he said gratefully, and drank carefully so the water wouldn't run out of the corners of his mouth and be wasted. "God always blesses those who are generous to a stranger."

Francis

"You must be Francis of Assisi," Layla said. "As we've traveled, we've heard people talking about you. It's wonderful that you sing the gospels in a language people can understand. We're all honored to meet you."

Francis looked embarrassed. He wasn't a man comfortable with praise. "I'm no one special, unless you believe that in God's eyes we're all special. Thank you again for the water. I hope to get to the village of Lauria before nightfall, and it's a long walk. I've been asked to help the people there celebrate Jesus' birthday. When I was in Lauria earlier in the year, I made a suggestion about celebrating the holiday that they said they might try, and I'm anxious to see if they've done it."

"What suggestion was that?" asked Attila, who was usually the last among us to warm to anyone he didn't know. Apparently, he approved of Francis and the way he cared for ordinary people.

"Will you walk with me a while as we talk?" Francis asked. "I'd welcome the company, and the story takes some time to tell. I have to be on my way, so if you want to hear it I'm afraid you'll have to come along."

We had no reason not to; our current plans were only to do more gift-giving in the same general area, and the village of Lauria would be as good a place as any other. So the six of us joined Francis on the road there. We had two donkeys laden with packs. One of these packs held our supplies; the rest were crammed with toys. Francis had the good manners not to ask what the donkeys carried. He himself had no pack animal, and in fact didn't even have a small bag to carry on his own shoulder. Francis trusted so much in the kindness of others that he never traveled with provisions. Instead, he counted on meeting people who would share their food with him.

It was a cool day, but sunny. As we walked, Francis told about what he hoped would happen that night in Lauria.

"I have thought for some time that the real circumstances of Jesus' birth are being forgotten," Francis explained. "In our churches now we see great paintings of Jesus rising to Heaven, and so we forget that he came into this world as the child of poor parents, and even was born, it's told, in a Bethlehem stable. I think it would comfort poor people today if they remembered that the baby Jesus was really one of them. Religion should be a source of comfort, don't you agree?

"Anyway, I suggested to the people of Lauria that they remember Jesus and his humble beginnings by building another stable and acting out the night of his birth, complete with cattle lowing and the donkey Mary rode tethered near the baby's bed, which would be blankets placed on straw just as it must have been in Bethlehem."

This nativity scene sounded like a sight well worth seeing. It was late afternoon before we got to Lauria. As we reached the village square, Francis gasped with surprise and delight. A life-size stable, or manger, as it was called in those days, had been built. A small water trough was inside, and cattle were drinking from it. Several villagers were bustling about, placing piles of straw and pounding on the manger's dirt floor with heavy sticks to flatten out lumps of clay.

"Brother Francis!" one of them called. "See, we've done what you asked. Tonight, we'll act out everything, with someone as Joseph, someone as Mary . . . all of it! Then tomorrow on the holy day you can lead us in prayer, and afterward we'll feast. This will be the best Christ's Day ever!" (The word "Christmas" still wasn't in wide use, except in England. Since 1038, people there had referred to their annual December 25 church service as "Cristes Maesse" or "Christ's Mass." This special name for a special day would gradually spread from England to the rest of the world with English explorers and traders.)

And, afterward, we all agreed it just might have been the best Christ's Day, or Christmas, that anyone anywhere ever enjoyed. The whole reenactment of the nativity, or birth scene, added a special meaning to Christmas Eve. The humble villagers of Lauria were reminded that Jesus came into this world poor, and that he lived as a simple man, not as some sort of royalty. Francis sang appropriate gospel verses in Italian. The six of us traveling with him were invited to stay with some of the villagers. Their cottages were small, but very clean.

The next morning all the people of Lauria gathered for a breakfast that would not have been anything special for rich people, but was undoubtedly splendid for them—hot fresh bread, assorted fruit,

bits of cold meat, and especially delicious pastries. The gingerbread
was the best I'd ever tasted, and since everyone was so generous in
urging me to have more I kept gobbling it until Layla pointedly told
everyone that her husband Nicholas was getting much too fat.

After the meal came the presents. These, of course had been cus-
tomary ever since the first Saturnalia celebrations in Rome. Everyone had a little something for each member of his or her family, and
neighbors exchanged gifts as well. The gifts were really tokens, like
cut straw for brooms or small squares of leather for patching sandals. Still, everyone made a fuss over what he or she had received,
and there were hugs and loud expressions of thanks.

"Each person is so grateful for the gifts, yet they're just small
items anyone could acquire at any time of the year," Felix said quietly to Francis, who hadn't eaten much of the wonderful food, preferring to sit and happily watch the villagers rejoice over their
presents.

"It's not the value of the gift, but the philosophy of the giving
and receiving," Francis replied. "It's a hard world, all in all, and to
receive a present means someone else cares for you, that you're not
alone."

"I already know that," Felix said a little huffily, and I knew he
was thinking he'd been secretly giving gifts eight hundred years
before Francis had even been born. But Francis's words were further
proof, if we needed it, that he was someone who would perfectly
understand our mission. I'd been thinking since soon after we'd first
met Francis that it might be a good idea to invite him to join us. But
just as Charlemagne had his own job to do that was separate from
ours, so, I decided, did Francis. We ended up saying good-bye to him
that afternoon. He walked off toward another small village, while

we stayed one more night in Lauria, leaving before dawn. When the children of Lauria awoke that morning, they all found toys beside their bedding.

Two years passed; Francis's idea of a nativity scene to help celebrate December 25 spread quickly. A few villages had great debates about whether it was really proper to act out the night of Jesus' birth since the actors would be mere humans, while Jesus, Mary, and Joseph were holy. Other communities were so small and poor that sufficient wood and other building materials for a life-size manger couldn't be spared. So, many families made miniature mangers instead, and filled them with little clay or stick figures representing the baby, his parents, the animals, shepherds, even the three Magi, or Wise Men. The nativity scene custom then spread throughout the rest of Christian Europe; within two centuries, few households celebrated December 25 without one.

Then, in 1225, we happened upon Francis again, once more in a small Italian village, and once more just a few days prior to December 25. This time we met at a crossroads. He looked exactly the same as when we'd last seen him in Lauria, except perhaps a little more tired.

After hearty greetings, we suggested he join us along the roadside for a meal. Francis accepted, saying he hadn't eaten for almost two days.

"Sometimes the villages I come to are so poor I don't accept offers of food because I know none can really be spared," he explained. "Obviously, your group is especially blessed and always has enough to eat, if the waistlines of Felix and Nicholas are any proof."

We took out cheese, fruit, and bread. I was careful not to eat too much, feeling somewhat embarrassed by Francis's comment.

Felix, I noticed, felt no similar shame. He ate his share and most of mine, too.

"What have you been doing lately, Francis?" Layla asked. "Your idea of the manger scenes was certainly successful. We feel so lucky to have been part of the first one in Lauria."

"Would you like to be part of another first effort?" Francis asked. "I've been thinking more about December twenty-fifth celebrations, and it seems to me that music should be included, too. I've heard some church officials grumbling lately that there's too much drinking and other inappropriate behavior used to celebrate Christ's birthday. Well, ordinary people love to sing and dance, and their everyday lives are so busy that they can't indulge in these pleasures too often. Of course, they want to sing and dance whenever they have one of their rare chances to stop working and enjoy themselves! So I've been thinking it might be best for everyone if we found some way to connect celebrating Jesus' birth with songs as well as feasting and presents."

Francis paused to sip some water and swallow a few bites of cheese.

"Tell us more," urged Felix, who always liked to sing and dance. "I like this idea even more than the mangers."

"It involves carols," Francis explained. Now, in 1225 the word "carols" didn't mean what it does today. Medieval carols were dances in village streets. Flutes would be played to provide the proper music. The people who danced would join hands in a circle and move to the rhythm. Sometimes words would be sung, too.

"So there should be carols written that celebrate Jesus' birth," Francis said. "I have a few already prepared, just the parts of the new gospels dealing with Bethlehem, really. I've spent some time lately at the village of Banyoli. There are some brothers there who play flutes as well as the angels must in Heaven. We're going to attempt some carols at Banyoli's December twenty-fifth celebration. Would you like to come along and see what happens?"

Of course we wanted to come, and it was just as splendid a success as the nativity scenes had been. People laughed and danced and sang, all in celebration of Jesus being born, and somehow it seemed right that such joy should be part of their thanks for his birth.

"Feasts, presents, mangers, carols—what a very special occasion December twenty-fifth has become!" Arthur chuckled. "I believe I'll find myself looking forward to this day all during the rest of the year!"

"The most important thing is that people are being happy together," Francis emphasized. "For at least one day of the year, past quarrels are forgotten and strangers are greeted as friends."

The next morning we ate breakfast with Francis. He had plans to be in another village that night, singing the gospels in Italian. In the early light, I noticed how the lines around his eyes were much deeper, how his hands trembled just a little when he raised a crust of bread to his mouth.

"What's troubling you, Francis?" I asked. "For all the happiness you're bringing others, I sense you're not very happy yourself."

Francis shrugged. "It's just that often, now, people expect me to be able to do things I can't. I'm a man, a human being, no more than that, but I'll come to a village and find they've heard stories of how I've magically made the real manger fly to Italy from Bethlehem, or how I call down choirs of angels to sing the gospels with me. When they find I can't do those things, that all I have to offer is my own poor voice, well, sometimes I know they're disappointed. I gladly give all I can, but for many that isn't enough. I wanted to help bring about a world that treated every day as specially as December twenty-fifth, but I wonder if instead I'm not somehow ruining all the other days of the year."

Sitting beside me, Layla gave me a powerful poke in the ribs with her elbow. I grunted in surprise. Francis, lost in his sad thoughts, didn't seem to notice.

I leaned toward my wife and whispered, "What did you do that for?"

Layla whispered back, "Tell him everything, Nicholas! This is the right time."

"What about leaving him alone to accomplish his own mission?" I muttered.

"Maybe it's been accomplished; perhaps it's time to help him find another one," she replied.

I trusted Layla's instincts above those of all others. I asked Francis to postpone his travels for a day, and to walk out into the fields with me and my companions for a talk. We spent that day telling our story, which, since it involved ten centuries, took its usual long time to explain. Francis listened intently, looking especially amazed when we explained who Attila and Arthur really were. I spoke, Felix spoke, Layla added several comments; it was a lot for poor Francis to take in.

But he did, and he believed us, too. "In this great world, all things must be possible," he said. "Somehow I know I'm really talking to Saint Nicholas of Myra, and Attila the Hun, and Arthur, legendary High King of Britain. King Arthur, I've read of you just lately in Geoffrey Monmouth's *History of the Kings of Britain*!"

"I was only a tribal chief," Arthur said gently. "Don't believe everything you read. But in that sense, several of us here know what you mean when you say stories of what you've done are so exaggerated that no reality can measure up. Who wants to believe I was a war chief who lived in a straw and mud hut, when they can picture me sitting on a golden throne in imaginary Camelot?"

"We should get to the point," Layla interrupted. "Francis, you've done as much in a normal life as anyone could. Join us, and you'll have limitless time to do good deeds, but without the pressure of being recognized and expected to work miracles every day."

"I'm not sure I can," Francis said humbly. "I'm a simple priest; I don't think I will be able to live forever, or at least hundreds of more years."

"Well, why not try?" boomed Attila. "Nicholas's magic has somehow attached itself to us, too. If for some reason you join us and aren't as lucky, well, you haven't really lost anything, have you?"

And so Francis of Assisi was persuaded to join our band, and a wonderful addition he was, too. Above all we treasured his marvelous mind and his knack for understanding the simple needs of ordinary people. Determined to properly close out what he called his "mortal" life, Francis first returned to Assisi, where he arranged for trusted friends to announce he died unexpectedly while praying in the Portiuncula Chapel, his favorite church and the first headquarters of the Franciscan movement he founded.

After staying out of sight for a few months, during which he rested and regained much of the strength he'd lost earlier, Francis met us outside Rome. No one else paid any attention to the slight, smiling man in ragged robes and patched sandals. They would have been very surprised to learn he was the same Francis of Assisi who, just a year later, was named a saint by the church.

"Saint Francis and Saint Nicholas," Arthur laughed when the news of Francis's new title reached us. "I feel second-class because I was only supposed to be a king!"

"Are you convinced?" Marco Polo asked, looking over his shoulder to
the spot where Attila had been standing. But Attila wasn't there any longer;
panicked by the exploding gunpowder, he'd dived under a nearby cart.

FOURTEEN

Gunpowder, Chimneys, and Stockings

 oon after Francis joined us, many other things happened, and quickly, too. The world went through one of its periods of great change. Of course, some changes were more welcome than others.

In 1270, Europeans first heard about gunpowder. The Chinese had invented this explosive material much, much earlier, but since Europeans really didn't travel into China until the late 1200s, it took that long for the information to spread west. An Italian writer published a report on gunpowder he called "Book of Fires for Burning Enemies." While the rest of us thought this new thing called gunpowder sounded extremely dangerous, Arthur and Attila were curious to see how it really worked.

They got their chance twenty-five years later. While traveling in Venice, our party met a merchant-explorer who had just returned from a long series of adventures in China. The man's name was Marco Polo. Although he was constantly surrounded by people who wanted to hear more about the mysterious place where he'd been, we were lucky enough to catch up with him near a big house where he was staying. A friendly fellow, Marco Polo invited us all inside. When Arthur and Attila asked him about gunpowder, he took a small container from a wooden chest. Opening the container, he spilled some black smelly particles into their palms.

"That's gunpowder," Marco Polo said. "What do you think of it?"

"It looks like dirt," Attila said bluntly. "How can something like this burn with enough force to injure an enemy? What are you supposed to do, throw the powder on them, and then ask them to hold still while you build a fire to light it?"

Marco Polo grinned; obviously, he was used to doubters. "The powder is collected in containers," he explained. "The powder is packed in tightly and a twist of cloth or paper is forced into it, like a wick is used for a candle. This wick into the gunpowder is lit, and when the flame reaches the powder there is a loud explosion. The force of the explosion can be used to launch weapons at great speed and height."

"I can hardly believe it," Attila said, so to prove his point Marco Polo fashioned a small paper tube, stuffed gunpowder and a wick into it, led us back into the street, motioned for passersby to move away, and lit the wick. The subsequent loud crack hurt my ears; there was quite a lot of smoke, too, which stung my eyes.

"Are you now convinced?" Marco Polo asked, looking over his shoulder to the spot where Attila had been standing. But Attila wasn't there any longer. Panicked by the exploding gunpowder, he'd dived under a nearby cart.

Some of Marco Polo's route of travel in China and other countries.
He then returned to Venice.

"I hate to think what terrible injuries that gunpowder will inflict on brave soldiers and innocent people," Attila said sadly, after we'd helped him to his feet and brushed off the street dirt and straw that had stuck to his clothes.

We spent several more days in Marco Polo's company. He was an interesting person and told us many stories about China and the people who lived there. Felix thought we should ask Marco Polo to join us, and I almost did. But before I could make the suggestion, he told us he intended to stay in Venice and possibly fight for the city in a war he expected to occur between Venice and the neighboring city of Genoa.

"I wouldn't do that if I were you," cautioned Francis, who remembered his own experiences in a war between Italian cities, but

Marco Polo was determined to stay and fight. He ended up being captured and spent three years in a Genoa prison, where he wrote a book about his Chinese travels. The book was widely read. For the next five hundred years, it provided most of the information Europeans had about China, a country that rarely encouraged outsiders to come and visit.

We never had a chance to speak with Marco Polo again, but we'd have many more experiences with gunpowder. Attila's prediction was unfortunately correct. Almost immediately, nations outside of China began to use the new material in their wars. The earliest recorded instance was in 1304, when Arabs used gunpowder rammed into bamboo tubes to shoot arrows at enemies.

Other inventions were more welcome. Eyeglasses first appeared in Italy in 1286. By 1300 they were being manufactured in Marco Polo's home city of Venice. These eyeglasses used specially shaped lenses of glass, which were placed in frames and worn so that the lenses rested in front of each eye. If the shape of the lenses matched the weaknesses of the eye, the person wearing the eyeglasses could see much more clearly. Felix, Arthur, Francis, Attila, Dorothea, Layla, and I all tried on eyeglasses, and Felix and I were astonished to each find a pair that helped us see better. We purchased several pairs and carried them with us on our travels. The lenses of these

I try eyeglasses for
the first time

glasses were convex, thicker in the middle than at the top and bottom. They helped us see things that were close up, such as writing on pages. Concave lenses, thinner in the middle than at top and bottom, were only invented a century later. These helped people see things better that were far away. And it was only in the late 1700s that a future friend of ours in America, a fellow named Ben Franklin, invented bifocal lenses, ones that were half for farsightedness and half for nearsightedness.

It was about 1300 that a long period of about four hundred years called the Renaissance began. This was a very welcome time when people became more interested in art and music—things that enriched lives instead of threatening them. Painters and composers got some of the glory that previously belonged only to generals. To put it simply, the world started to become more civilized.

This didn't mean that things were perfect. Wars continued, and there still wasn't much knowledge about medicine, which meant diseases could and did spread widely. How many people were fed still depended mostly on the weather—when seasons were moderate, farmers could grow plenty of crops. But let one winter be especially severe or a spring go by without enough rain, and starvation was always possible. From 1314 through 1317, there was a great famine. England, Ireland, and Poland were especially hard hit. Then in 1347, a terrible disease killed almost one-third of all the people in Europe; later on, in history books, this plague was called "The Black Death."

But, as with time itself, disease didn't seem to touch us. We all remained healthy, and did everything we could to ease suffering when we found it—and we still found it everywhere.

"The good that is happening will last longer than the bad things," Layla said firmly. "At last, people are using some of their energy in positive ways. What's the game that was just invented in Germany, and that we all played there? The one that was so enjoyable?"

"Bowling," Felix said. Bowling did seem like lots of fun. To play, ten wooden bottle-shaped pins were set up in a sort of triangle, and people would roll wooden balls and try to knock down as many of the pins as they could. It took a long time to play, however, mostly because setting the pins back up was a lot harder than knocking them down.

"The greatest invention in history will be the one that picks up the bowling pins for the players," Attila grumbled. "And I'm not saying that just because all of you beat me, either."

"You tried to roll the ball too hard," Arthur said helpfully. "Bowling is a game of skill, not strength. You didn't bowl well for the same reason your Huns never could defeat the Romans. You just went into battle without any real plan, and they thought things through before they fought."

"I didn't notice your British tribes doing any better against the Saxons," Attila shot back. "Don't tell me about fighting, and don't tell me about bowling, either." He and Arthur glared at each other.

"It's ridiculous for you two to argue about a friendly game of bowling, let alone battles that occurred almost a thousand years ago," I said. "Instead, why don't we think about making miniature bowling games to give to children? Arthur, you figure out a way to make the small wooden balls, and, Attila, you decide how we should carve the pins." It was always a simple thing to make them stop arguing. Like the rest of us, they enjoyed making and giving gifts more than anything else.

The 1350s saw widespread use of another relatively new invention, and one that would become part of our legend. One night in France, Felix and I crept into a small country village with several sacks of toys we meant to distribute to the children who lived there—maybe fifty children in all, living in two dozen cottages. We'd never been to this village, but Layla and Dorothea had visited the day before. They'd told us how many children lived there and how many presents we should pack for our gift-giving.

Felix and I quietly approached the village, taking care not to wake up the many dogs sleeping nearby. Interestingly, dogs rarely bothered us, anyway. They always seemed to sense we came for a good purpose, not to rob or otherwise hurt anyone they loved.

We neared the first cottage; I was reaching into my sack for two wooden tops. Layla had said two young brothers lived there. As I took out the tops, Felix suddenly hissed, "What's that?"

"Where?" I asked, worried someone had seen us.

"That, that—well, that thing on the side of the cottage!" Felix spluttered. I looked where he was pointing, and there attached to one outer

A family's stockings hanging by the fireplace

wall was a squarish-looking stone structure tall enough to stick above the roof. Little swirls of woodsmoke were coming out of the top of it.

After a few moments of thought, I whispered, "That must be one of those newfangled chimneys we've been hearing about. You know, with fires built in the bottom of them to provide homes with light and warmth. That part is known as the fireplace. Then the smoke from the fire comes out the top of the chimney and doesn't settle back inside the house."

"Amazing," Felix answered. We both stood looking in wonder at this chimney. Then he added, "Well, let's go inside."

We rarely had any trouble getting into a house or cottage. Fancy locks for doors hadn't been invented yet. Later on, when they were, Attila proved masterful at teaching the rest of us how to open them. So Felix and I easily opened the wooden door of the cottage and slipped inside.

As with most cottages in small European villages of this time, there was only one large room. Seven people were sleeping in it, apparently the two parents, the two children, a grandmother and a grandfather and an aunt. Often lots of relatives lived together, for shelter was scarce. We quickly identified the straw bedding where the two boys slept, but before we left our gifts beside them we found ourselves drawn back to the marvelous fireplace. A tiny blaze burned at the bottom of it.

"Look at how the smoke is drawn straight up," Felix muttered. "If you weren't so wide in the middle, you could get into houses just by getting on the roof and jumping down the chimneys."

It was rare that we ever talked while inside a house, for fear of waking someone up, but I couldn't let this insult pass.

"You're quite wide yourself, my friend, so don't mock my waist-line," I said. "Besides, if I jumped down the chimney I'd burn my feet on the fire when I landed! Still, you've given me an idea. Look, for instance, at how the whole family's stockings have been hung up by the front of the fireplace to dry in front of the flames while everyone sleeps. Remember my story of leaving my first gifts ever in the stockings of Shem's daughters? Let's leave these toys in the stockings of the boys. They won't burn—the fire isn't that large or hot—and in the morning maybe the family will think the mysterious gift-giver came down the chimney, just as you suggested!"

So we put toys in the stockings and hurried on to the next cottage, and the next, and the next, and the next. In each one with a chimney we found stockings drying in front of the fire, and we always left our gifts in the smaller stockings worn by the children.

After sunup, Felix and I made a point of going back to the village and listening to the excited gossip there. Everyone was talking about how all the children had found toys in their stockings that morning, and how whoever had left the toys must have come down the chimneys without being burned by the flames in the fireplaces.

"Surely whoever gave these gifts must have great magical powers!" declared one elderly woman, and everyone around her nodded in agreement. Felix and I grinned and hurried back to our camp to tell the tale to the others. Forever afterward, in houses with chimneys, we always left our gifts in stockings by fireplaces, if the children in those families had left their stockings hanging there.

To everyone's joy, Attila and Dorothea met and hired perhaps the finest
craftsman who ever lived—Willie Skokan, a short, wiry fellow who
could take a sharp knife, a bit of wood, some string and paint,
and literally create any toy imaginable.

FIFTEEN

At Court
with Columbus

ntil about 1400, our group of seven traveled everywhere together. Felix, Arthur, Attila, Dorothea, Francis, Layla, and I were good, close friends. But as the world changed, the way we did things had to change, too. We began to feel the frustration of not being able to be in enough places at once. Since we were always going someplace or another, there was never any opportunity to settle in one spot for a while and concentrate only on making toys of the highest quality. This especially frustrated Arthur and Attila, who were by far the finest craftsmen among us, better even than Felix, who himself was much better than me. At the same time, Layla and Dorothea constantly suggested we try to make some specific toys for girls, as well. They felt tops and the like were mostly favorites of boys.

Finally, Arthur and Attila came to me with a suggestion: For the first time, they said, the group should divide, with some of us trav-

eling and gift-giving, and the others remaining in one place to concentrate on crafting as many fine toys as possible.

"And the ones who travel can be constantly on the lookout for
new places where gifts should be given," Arthur said. "That's obviously the role for you, Nicholas, and for Francis and Felix and Layla.
You're the ones who really enjoy the traveling. As for me, I'm never
entirely happy unless I'm in England, and Attila longs to remain in
Germany, and Dorothea wants to be there with him. So let us go to
the places where we love to be the most, and once there we'll do
what we love doing the most, which is making toys."

It was soon agreed. Arthur would set up toy-making operations in
London, and Attila and Dorothea in the German city of Nuremberg.
Quietly, they'd acquire property and build workshops, then recruit
the finest craftsmen they could find. Half the toys manufactured in
the workshops would be sold in city markets to raise the money necessary to pay the workers' salaries and buy materials. The other half
would be turned over to those of us continuing the gift-giving.

Felix and Francis went to Germany with Attila and Dorothea to
help get everything started in Nuremberg. Layla and I accompanied
Arthur to London, and a very unhappy place we found it. The London streets were filthy; people threw garbage everywhere. England
was involved in ongoing wars with France and also in its own civil
wars, with rival families taking turns claiming the English throne.

"How can you be happy here, with so much fighting going on?"
Layla asked Arthur.

He shrugged. "It's my home," he said simply. Almost one thousand years after he'd given up fighting the Saxons to join us, Arthur
still had the force of character necessary to be a good leader. He
quickly found a dozen fine craftsmen to come to work in the new toy
factory, men and women skilled in carving and sewing and painting.

They were delighted to have a chance to earn their livings in such a happy way.

Arthur's toy factory was operating within six months, and Attila's in Nuremberg opened a few weeks after that. Felix, Francis, Layla, and I—who were left to do the traveling and gift-giving—missed being with our good friends very much. But there was comfort in knowing they were happy to be in permanent homes, and a few times every year we'd go to one toy factory or the other to replenish our supply of gifts, and then we'd have happy reunions with them.

Layla took special pride in Dorothea's role at the Nuremberg toy factory. Dorothea insisted on hiring several special German craftsmen herself and having them do nothing but create wonderful wooden dolls. Nobody knew for certain where the word "doll" came from, although Dorothea always believed it was based on the German word "tocke," which literally means a small block of wood. This is what dolls were carved from in those days.

To everyone's joy, Attila and Dorothea met and hired perhaps the finest craftsman who ever lived—Willie Skokan, a short wiry fellow who could take a sharp knife, a bit of wood, some string and paint, and literally create any toy imaginable. It became Willie's job not only to make toys, but to invent them. Some of his first inventions in Nuremberg were small wooden models of Noah's Ark, complete with tiny animal figures to move in and out of the boat; toy musical instruments, flutes and recorders that children could blow into and compose tunes; wooden puppets, marvelously jointed and able to do all sorts of tricks for those who pulled their strings; dollhouses for dolls to live in; and, finally, toy weapons, blunt-edged wooden swords and bow and arrows.

These last toys worried the rest of us. We wanted children to play with the gifts we gave so they'd forget the bad things in life, not pretend to be doing the bad things themselves. But Willie, in his unique, halting way, explained why he thought someday children would no longer find toy weapons interesting.

Willie Skokan

"Children follow the examples of their parents," he told Layla and me one night at his cottage in Nuremberg as we ate a plain dinner of toasted bread and cheese. Willie could build elaborate toys, but his personal tastes were always quite simple. Once, when asked his philosophy of life, he replied, "Moderation in all things." At dinner we debated whether war toys were appropriate for gift-giving. "There's a lot of fighting in this world, and when children play they often reflect real life," Willie said.

"But if they didn't have toys that reminded them of violence, maybe they wouldn't grow up to be violent themselves," Layla argued.

Willie looked thoughtful and took a moment before replying. "What we should do is hope that grown-ups learn to set better examples. When they give up their instruments of war, children will no longer want toy weapons." And from that time we kept making and giving pretend swords and bows, and later toy guns and rifles, to the children who wanted them.

The 1400s had other moments of special significance, and as usual some were better than others. Besides the wars, the saddest time for me was in 1444, which was when the ship fleet of Henry the Navigator began to bring captured African natives to Portugal, where these innocent African men and women were sold as slaves in the market-place. In previous history, and in the centuries yet to come, there had been and would be nothing more disgusting than some human beings believing they had the right to own others.

We made special efforts to bring gifts to slave children, but this was often quite difficult. Slaveowners guarded their so-called "human property" all through the night hours to be sure none of them escaped. Only rarely could we elude detection by these guards and get into slave quarters to leave our presents.

Some of Willie Skokan's toys

In the later 1400s, Francis had the urge to spend time in the Western European kingdoms of Aragon and Castile, which eventually would be combined into the nation of Spain. These lands were, in many ways, the cultural and political centers of Europe. It was important that we knew everything happening there. So, while Felix, Layla, and I concentrated on central Europe and England, Francis spent several years getting to know Ferdinand and Isabella, the king and queen of Aragon and Castile. Eventually in the spring of 1492, Francis wrote to me in care of Attila's Nuremberg toy factory, asking my permission to tell the king and queen about us and our mission. Isabella in particular, Francis said, might be persuaded to give us financial help in much the same way that Charlemagne had nearly seven hundred years earlier.

I wrote back telling Francis that I trusted his judgment. He was right; Isabella was thrilled to learn about us and our mission. Ferdinand was less enthusiastic. He wanted to use his government's money for wars. Francis wrote me again, asking me to come to their court and meet Isabella for myself.

"Though she respects her husband the king, she also will do things she believes to be right whether he approves of them or not," Francis wrote.

Able to travel at ten times the speed of normal mortals, Layla, Felix, and I were Isabella's guests less than a week after we received Francis's letter.

The three of us were introduced to Isabella by Francis in the privacy of the queen's chambers. I wanted to like Isabella, but I found it difficult. She had decorated her rooms with the most expensive furnishings available. We could have made toys for every child in her kingdom for much less than she'd spent on curtains and chandeliers. Also, Isabella had a rather forceful way of speaking, usually interrupting whoever was talking to her and immediately forming rigid opinions about everything.

"So you're Saint Nicholas himself," she said immediately, her voice so loud I feared everyone in the castle might have heard her. "Did you really work all those miracles, the saving of sinking ships and so forth?"

"I've only heard the same stories that you have, Your Majesty," I said politely. "As I'm sure Francis has told you, my time is spent giving gifts to children, and nothing more heroic than that."

"Exactly why I like you!" the queen announced. "I, too, am very fond of children. Perhaps you would like to give a gift to my daughter Catherine."

"I doubt your daughter needs our modest gifts," I replied, thinking to myself that this woman didn't really understand what we did at all. I caught a glimpse of Francis standing just behind Isabella;

when his eyes met mine, he grimaced and shrugged. I must admit, though, that later in our visit to Isabella when we met Princess Catherine, I felt so sorry for the child that I wished we had brought something to give her.

Catherine was a very solemn girl who looked much more like her father than her mother, and King Ferdinand was big-nosed and jut-chinned, rather than handsome. It was quite clear Catherine was going to be one of those unfortunate princesses who someday would be married off by her parents to create some sort of political alliance with another country and its ruler. As it turned out, in 1501, when she was sixteen, Catherine's parents ordered her to marry Prince Arthur of England, who was the oldest son of King Henry VII. This marriage had a great impact on our mission, although the proper time to tell more about it comes later in this story.

In any event, Queen Isabella pronounced herself truly committed to helping us. King Ferdinand would not allow her to give us money from the national treasury, she said, so instead she would simply give us all her jewelry, which we could sell for a great deal of money.

"It was rather a hard choice about who should get this jewelry, you or that Italian captain who also has been asking us for financial help," Isabella added. "What was his name, again, Francis? You met him a few weeks ago."

"Christopher Columbus," Francis added helpfully. "He said he thinks, or rather he knows, a quick trade route to the Indies and Japan could be found simply by sailing directly west instead of cir-cling east around the Cape as the trading ships do now. An interest-ing fellow, really. I'm sorry your decision to help us comes at his expense."

Isabella told us we would have to remain at the castle for a few weeks while she collected all her necklaces, earrings, rings, and other jeweled finery. She kept some items at other castles and had loaned others to family and friends. When I told her it probably wouldn't be necessary for us to be given every item she owned, Isabella just laughed and said it was always easy for queens to get all the jewelry they wanted. After she gave us what she had, she'd just tell rich noblemen who wanted the king's favor to give her more.

So we waited, and on the third day after we'd met Isabella, we were walking in the courtyard when Francis said, "Look, over there. That fellow is Columbus, the Italian captain I told you about."

Columbus was older than I'd expected, certainly more than forty. His hair had turned gray and, like many people of that time, his teeth were yellow and nasty-looking. But he had a nice smile, though a sad one.

"I'm told by the queen that there's no longer a chance she can help me because she's going to give her jewelry to you," Columbus said, sounding depressed but not angry at us. "She won't say why you need the jewels, but I suppose it's for some fine purpose. I have a final appointment with King Ferdinand this afternoon, and I'll ask him one last time for money for my voyages. If he refuses, as I'm certain he will, I suppose I'll have to go back home. I've already been turned down by the King of Portugal, and by every nobleman in Italy."

"Perhaps King Ferdinand will decide to help you after all," I said cheerfully. "Francis has told us about your idea of a new way to sail to Japan or the Indies."

"It's not just an idea to make me rich, you know," Columbus said. "Everyone would benefit, even the Japanese and Indians. We have goods they want, and we want theirs. Craftsmen in every country in Europe would be able to sell more, and thus make more profits. People could live better. Fewer children would go hungry."

After we left Columbus, the four of us talked about what he had said. "Do you really think he can reach Japan or the Indies just by sailing west?" I asked Francis. "There are still many people who think ships going west will just fall off the edge of the world."

"The oceans have been sailed enough for anyone intelligent to know there are no edges to fall off," Francis replied. "I do wish Columbus would get his chance. If he did, I'd like to go with him. We need to know more about Japan and the Indies, Nicholas. No doubt there are many children there who need gifts, too."

The more we discussed it, the more it became clear that Christopher Columbus was just as deserving of Isabella's help as we were. This wasn't convenient for us, of course. We needed all the money we could get. Every day, each of us felt frustrated because we never had enough gifts for all the deserving children we wanted to please. Anyone trying to do good things has to believe in the cause being served, and that can make it easy to forget that others are trying to do good things, too—different things, perhaps, but still important.

So, that evening we went back to Isabella to ask if she might spare a few items of jewelry for Columbus after all. At first she was surprised we didn't want it all for ourselves, but eventually agreed to spare him enough to buy and outfit no more than three small ships. Francis ran to find Columbus and tell him the good news, only to be informed the captain had left court an hour earlier, headed home to Italy after King Ferdinand had refused his final request for money. Undaunted, Francis borrowed a mule and tracked Columbus down, bringing him back to court for a private meeting with the rest of us and Queen Isabella. When she told him she would finance his trip, he began to offer his thanks. Isabella interrupted him.

"There are conditions, of course, Captain Columbus," she said firmly. "Most important, whatever new lands you might find must be claimed in the name of King Ferdinand and myself. Second, we must receive nine-tenths of all the wealth you find. And third, my friend Francis must sail with you on this adventure."

Except for Francis, we all looked surprised. Columbus was so pleased to get his money that he was glad to have Francis come along, especially when Isabella explained he was an Italian priest. Columbus was very religious and told Francis it would be an honor to have him aboard.

Isabella collected her jewelry and divided it between us and Columbus. The captain then bought three ships, which he named the *Niña*, the *Pinta*, and the *Santa María*. On August 3, 1492, he sailed from the harbor of Palos; Felix, Layla, and I stood on the dock waving good-bye to Francis.

Columbus's three ships—the *Niña*, *Pinta*, and *Santa María*

Later, Francis told us colorful tales of the trip. Columbus did not turn out to be an especially good leader of men. Several times, his crews were ready to mutiny. But more than two months after leaving Palos, they sighted land on the western horizon. Poor Columbus thought this land might be Japan, but it turned out to be one of a series of sandy islands inhabited by native tribes who certainly weren't Japanese. Always ready to fool himself and others with grand exaggeration, Columbus instantly decided he must have reached the Indies. As he had promised, he claimed the first island, which he called San Salvador, in the names of Ferdinand and Isabella.

He also called the natives "Indians." Columbus then ordered his ships to sail a bit farther, and they discovered and claimed several other islands in the next few days. One of these islands, which Columbus named "Juana," would eventually be known as Cuba. Columbus and his crew were shocked to see natives on this island smoking a dried plant. This was the first time Europeans had seen tobacco.

Columbus didn't turn out to be a very good sailor, either. On the night of December 24, he wrecked the *Santa María* on another new island, one he named Hispaniola. Today it is home to Haiti and the Dominican Republic.

"On the night of that shipwreck, after all the sailors were safe and as many goods as possible salvaged from the wreckage, I reminded Captain Columbus that it was Christmas Eve," Francis said. "I asked his permission to lead the sailors in a mass honoring Christ's birth. Although he was already losing himself in dreams of gold and glory, the captain said I could. I felt special sensations during the mass, Nicholas. It's not quite time yet, but you should mark my words. Much of our future and this mission of gift-giving lies in the New World. You'll have to go there and see for yourself."

"Perhaps so," I answered. "But before I set foot on a ship, I'll want to see what happens to Columbus and the rest of the explorers who'll undoubtedly follow him there. For now, we have enough work to do in the countries we already know about."

The New World did, in fact, turn out to be a glorious place, but Columbus himself didn't come to a glorious end. In March 1493, he returned from his first voyage to promise Ferdinand and Isabella that the lands he had claimed for them were full of gold and other valuable things. They sent him back three more times, but he didn't find any gold to bring them. Columbus was disgraced, and he died a very poor, unhappy man.

Francis didn't return to the New World on any of Columbus's last three voyages. Instead, he rejoined Felix, Layla, and me. The jewelry we'd received from Isabella was used by Arthur and Attila to expand their toy factories. Soon we had toys for almost every child in Europe and England, with some left over. We decided we should have a regular schedule to distribute them, and this decision led us into the next phase of our mission.

Whenever possible, presents were placed in stockings hung to dry by
the fireplace. This quickly caused a new flurry of myths about how Saint
Nicholas must prefer coming down the chimneys to any other way of
entering a home, and how children wanting to be certain of gifts
should hang up their stockings there on the appropriate night.

SIXTEEN

The Christmas Legend
of Saint Nicholas

ver since I started giving gifts back in Patara and Myra, people told stories about the mysterious person who came at night to leave presents for children. Over the centuries, as the territory where I gave gifts and the number of those gifts grew, so did the myths. It wasn't until about 1500, though, that the gift-giver was identified as me, or rather as Saint Nicholas.

Although we hadn't realized this at the time, it was inevitable at least some of the truth would become widely known after Arthur and Attila opened their toy factories and hired staff to work in them. Back then, simply the presence of factories that only made toys was unusual enough to arouse local interest, and, try as Arthur and Attila might, there were workers who learned something of what we did and couldn't resist telling family and friends. In centuries to come, some companies would require employees to sign "secrecy agreements," where they promised not to tell anyone else about the work they did. But in 1500, that hadn't been thought of yet.

A few very trusted workers knew everything: Willie Skokan, for instance, occasionally would come with Felix, Francis, Layla, and me when we delivered toys he had made. Willie wanted to watch children at play with their gifts. He would take notes on any problems they had with the toys, and then try to fix these design flaws when he got back to the Nuremberg factory.

At any rate, once the first Saint Nicholas tale was told there was no stopping the story from spreading. People seemed relieved to have a name by which to identify the mysterious gift-giver they'd been wondering about for so long. From Rome to London, and in every city and village in between, children began to hope they'd get a nighttime visit from Saint Nicholas.

"This is going to be very awkward," I told Layla one night as we sat by a tiny campfire in the hill country of France. Felix and Francis were asleep, rolled up in their blankets as close to the warmth of the fire as they could get without setting their bedding ablaze. "I understand many children now pray at bedtime that Saint Nicholas will visit while they sleep and bring them something. I certainly don't want to disappoint anyone. What are we going to do?"

As always, Layla's commonsense approach to problems was helpful.

"You know that for some time we've been thinking about picking just a few very special nights each year for the gift-giving," she reminded me. "That way we can spend most of our time preparing the toys and choosing which children should receive them. We'll recruit more people to help deliver the gifts on these nights. That way, we'll be better organized and more children can wake up to delightful surprises."

"How will we find the right people to help with the gift-giving?" I wondered. "And how will we choose the special nights?"

Layla favored me with the sort of lovingly impatient look wives use when their husbands ask especially silly questions.

"Somehow, Nicholas, when you are concerned, things simply happen because they need to," she said. "When you needed Felix, you found him. When you needed me, you found me. The same is true of Attila and Dorothea and Arthur and Francis and Willie Skokan. The right people will find us. As for the nights to choose, well, I think we already know the most important one."

And, of course, we did. Christmas had become an almost universal day for exchanging gifts. What better time for children to receive our gifts, too?

"For reasons of time and convenience, in some countries we could choose other dates associated with Christ's birth and presents," I mused, suddenly inspired. "For instance, in some places gifts are given on January sixth, the day the three Wise Men are supposed to have arrived in Bethlehem and offered their presents to the baby Jesus. So there are two dates. Don't you think we need at least one more?"

We did, and, as Layla had guessed, that day was chosen for us. December 6, the anniversary of my supposed death, had been declared "Saint Nicholas Day" by the church. As soon as my name was connected with the mysterious gift-giving, families in some countries assumed I would come visit their children on that day instead of Christmas.

It took a few dozen years for us to arrange this new schedule. Eventually a plan evolved where Arthur and helpers would distribute gifts in England and the British Isles; Attila and Dorothea and assistants in Germany, France, and the European "middle countries"; Willie Skokan and helpers in Eastern Europe; Francis and associates in Spain, Portugal, and Western Europe; Felix and helpers in Scandinavia; Layla and helpers in Italy; and me assisting wherever I liked, working with one group one year and with another the next. Everyone went in Saint Nicholas costume, the traditional red robes trimmed with white that I had worn in my days as a bishop. They also glued on white beards to match mine, and Felix began the rude custom of stuffing a pillow under the belt of his robes—to imitate, he said, my "considerable" waistline.

Traveling faster than normal mortals could imagine, the various groups moved from city to village, from house to cottage, leaving gifts inside for the children who lived there. Whenever possible, presents were placed in stockings hung to dry by fireplaces. This quickly caused a new flurry of myths about how Saint Nicholas must prefer coming down chimneys to any other way of entering a home, and how children wanting to be certain of gifts should hang up their stockings there on the appropriate night.

It came as a welcome surprise that some parents, who hadn't before now, began using these special nights of December 25 and January 6 to give their children gifts, too. We might leave a doll for a little girl, and on that same night her mother and father might add a new dress, pieces of fruit, and perhaps even some candy.

The helpers we recruited came from all sorts of places, and from all kinds of professions. They were good-hearted men and women, sworn to secrecy, and people we somehow knew we could trust not to talk out of turn. Many helped us for a few years; some assisted us for decades, and a special few became part of our core group and stopped aging altogether, just as we had.

Even as our ranks grew and we were able to distribute more toys to more children, the quality of the toys we gave improved as well.

One of our finest new companions came to us from Italy in 1519. Leonardo da Vinci was the greatest painter of the time, and his *Mona Lisa* might be the most famous painting ever. It is still on display to the public in Paris's Louvre museum.

Francis had first met Leonardo in Milan, Italy, in the late 1400s, and kept in touch with him after that. Leonardo's style of painting was quite unique; he liked to use dark colors as backgrounds, believing this made light colors stand out better. Leonardo also was a great scientist. He

Leonardo da Vinci

filled whole notebooks with ideas for flying machines and boats that moved underwater. But in 1519, he told Francis he was tired of being such a public figure, saying, "The greatest artists work in private." Very soon Francis helped spirit Leonardo away from France, where he had been living, to Arthur's toy factory in London. Almost immediately, Leonardo came up with wonderful new ways to paint faces on dolls. He and Willie Skokan would meet once or twice a year to invent new toys. It was a happy time for Leonardo—indeed, it was a happy time for all of us.

"I believe we have finally done everything necessary," I told Felix one afternoon after we'd spent most of the day visiting Arthur in London. For a change the city seemed almost clean, and it was a fine, sunny spring day. "The factories here and in Germany are producing all the toys we need, we have special days to distribute our gifts, and since it's spring, with winter so far away, we can even relax a little and simply enjoy ourselves."

I should have known better. Life is never as uncomplicated as we'd prefer. Even as Felix and I chatted, a German priest named Martin Luther was breaking away from the Catholic church because he didn't agree with some church teachings. Because Luther's followers were said to be protesting, they eventually became known as "Protestants." European Christians no longer all belonged to the Catholic church.

There were religious changes in England, too. Little Princess Catherine of Aragon had, of course, grown up to marry Prince Arthur of England in 1501. Prince Arthur was expected to become England's king, but the poor fellow died unexpectedly before he ever had a chance to inherit the throne of his father, King Henry VII. Arthur's younger brother Henry became the new heir, and in 1509 Catherine had to marry Henry when he became king.

It wasn't a very happy marriage; Catherine was much older than Henry VIII, and by 1527 he wanted to divorce her. The Catholic church wouldn't allow the divorce; while Henry was arguing with church officials in Rome, he met a woman named Anne Boleyn and decided to marry her. Kings usually do what they want, and Henry ordered the English church to break away from the Catholic church. His new Church of England allowed Henry to divorce Catherine and marry Anne. This second marriage wasn't happy, either; Henry ended up getting married six different times. But the result for Christians in England was that, while Henry was king, they weren't encouraged to worship as Catholics anymore.

After Henry VIII died in 1547, his daughter Mary became queen and ruled England. She wanted everyone to become Catholics again.

Eleven years later Mary died and her sister Elizabeth became queen. She was a Protestant. The whole issue of religion, in England and in Europe, became quite confused.

This confusion affected our mission very much. I always loved children of all religious faiths and backgrounds, but the mythical Saint Nicholas who was supposed to give toys was traditionally a part of the Catholic church. People thought Saint Nicholas might only give toys to Catholic families. When our gift-giving continued as usual in every country regardless of whether children receiving them were Protestants or Catholics, the stories about who was giving the presents began to change.

For instance, Catholic saints weren't welcome in the England of Queen Elizabeth I, so parents began telling their children about "Father Christmas," who came down chimneys on Christmas Eve after everyone was asleep and filled the stockings of children who'd been good throughout the year. In France, the same mission was carried out by "Père Noel," and so on until each country seemed to have a different idea about who gave children presents and the nights on which he or she did it. You notice I say "he or she." In Italy, children began to believe that Befana, a very old woman, brought them their presents. Some Italian parents even told their children that Befana was a friendly witch.

Truthfully, it didn't matter to us what name this mysterious gift-giver was given, or what he or she was supposed to look like. We wanted to help children be happy. If that meant being Saint Nicholas in Belgium, and leaving gifts there on December 6, then being Father Christmas in England on December 25 and Befana in Italy on January 6, well, that was all right. Layla was especially pleased about the Befana tale, and insisted on dressing up in old robes and distributing the presents in Italy herself.

Sometimes it took a while for countries to separate our gift-giving from the religious purpose of Christmas, which of course was and is to celebrate the birth of Jesus. We never intended to interfere with that much more important part of the Christmas season. Rather, we wanted to add to it.

In Germany, for instance, parents told children that Saint Nicholas came on December 6, and that the Christ Child brought more gifts on December 25. "Christkind" was the German name for him. As years passed, that name began to be pronounced "Kris Kringle," by German settlers in other parts of the world, especially in America. German children today still expect their Christmas presents from the Christkind, who is usually accompanied by little gnomish helpers.

We heard all of these tales and considered them carefully before deciding on one simple rule. In each country, we would gladly take on whatever identity its children preferred. We would leave presents for children in every home where we were welcome. In a few cases, we learned that parents did not want us to come, and we regretfully avoided those houses.

Wars continued to trouble us. Our powers were always weakened whenever there was fighting nearby. Children whose countries were at war often had to do without gifts from us. It seemed like an unfair penalty for them, and our greatest pleasure was being able to return to these countries and give gifts there when the fighting was over.

As the 1500s passed and the 1600s began, we continued our mission in Europe and England. But reports continued to arrive from what everyone thought of as the New World. Columbus had been the first captain to sail across the Atlantic Ocean and claim land for Spain. England and France were among the other countries to hire explorers whose job was to establish settlements in the New World and bring back any treasure they might find.

"The biggest treasure in the New World is going to be the land itself," Francis kept insisting. "It's a special place, Nicholas, and one day it's going to be full of special people. When will you go there to see for yourself? We'll take care of things in the Old World for you while you're away."

I resisted the trip for quite a while. There was still so much work to do in England and Europe. It was especially enjoyable now to see new Christmas customs being developed—people in Germany decorating Christmas trees, for instance. Keeping green boughs during winter had long been traditional in many parts of the world—the idea was that these cheerful decorations promised spring would come again. But the Germans were the ones who connected this longtime belief to Christmas around the year 1500. Legend, which is almost always interesting but not always accurate, indicates the great German Martin Luther took some fresh evergreens into his home on Christmas, and after that, his friends and followers began to do the same.

But in the early 1600s, such lovely new Christmas traditions hadn't yet made their way across the Atlantic Ocean. It was reported that settlers in the New World were having hard times of it. They suffered from bad weather, strange diseases, and simple loneliness for the families and friends they had to leave behind. One complete English settlement called Roanoke simply disappeared.

"You know you want to go across the ocean and bring Christmas comfort to those suffering people," Layla scolded me one morning. "Arthur writes from London that some people calling themselves the Saints are going to sail to the New World in a ship called the *Mayflower*. Why not sail with them?"

"Will you come, too?" I asked.

"I think I'd better stay behind and make sure things run smoothly here," Layla replied. "Don't look so sad at the thought! It won't hurt us to be apart for a little while—after all, we've been married for over a thousand years!"

"I'll need someone to help me," I pleaded.

"Well, then, take Felix," Layla suggested. "It's been centuries since the two of you were out on your own together. It will almost be like a vacation for you."

So Felix and I went to London, where we met William Brewster, the leader of the Saints. He told us his group was leaving England because they weren't allowed to worship as they pleased, and that they called themselves Saints because they were willing to suffer to enjoy freedom of religion.

"We have exactly one hundred passengers, and one-third are part of our group," Brewster explained. "The others are craftsmen and physicians and such, who will be needed to help us establish our new colony. How could the two of you help out if we let you join us?"

"Well, I'm very good at carving wood and fixing things," Felix said quickly. "As for my friend Nicholas, well, he's a hard worker, if not a good one."

I was offended by Felix's remark and became even more offended when Brewster added, "Well, I can tell by his weight that he's at least good at eating. You might find yourself losing a few pounds in the New World, my friend!"

"I'll take my chances," I replied, feeling insulted.

Brewster agreed to let us come, so 102 passengers left England on the *Mayflower* in September 1620. All during the long, hard years ahead of them, these people called themselves Saints. It was only two hundred years later that historians renamed them "the Pilgrims."

"The so-called Saints certainly aren't living up to that name," Felix whispered to me, ducking a heavy plate some Saint had thrown at a non-Saint. "Nobody's gotten off this ship yet and already the trip seems to be a complete disaster."

SEVENTEEN

Hard Times in the
New World

he Saints and the rest of the 102 people bound for the New World were supposed to sail in two ships, the *Mayflower* and the *Speedwell*. But at the last minute, someone decided the *Speedwell* wasn't safe enough to cross the ocean. Felix and I thought this meant the trip would be delayed until another ship could be found, but instead all 102 of us were crowded into the ninety-foot-long *Mayflower*.

If everyone had acted pleasant it would have been hard enough to get along when we were packed so tightly together, but the thirty or so Saints weren't a very friendly group. They tried to keep separate from everyone else, which was practically impossible, and spent a lot of time criticizing the rest of us for not acting properly. What they meant by that was not doing everything exactly the way the Saints wanted. Several times there almost were fights. At one point during the voyage everyone was asked to sign an agreement to create a fair government when we landed, so that there would be reasonable laws for all of us to follow, Saints and non-Saints alike. Everyone couldn't wait for the day that we arrived at our destination, which was supposed to be near the area in Virginia where, in 1607, Captain John Smith of Britain had founded Jamestown, the first permanent British colony in the land most Europeans were already calling "America."

Well, we only missed landing in Virginia by hundreds of miles. Instead of sailing into a friendly harbor, the *Mayflower* ended up on the coastal rocks of Plymouth, Massachusetts, well to the north. Most passengers had already been in very bad moods, and this made them feel even worse. Everyone started accusing everyone else of all sorts of things.

"The so-called Saints certainly aren't living up to their name," Felix whispered to me, ducking a heavy plate some Saint had thrown at a non-Saint. "Nobody's gotten off this ship yet and already the trip seems to be a complete disaster."

William Brewster and another Saint leader, William Bradford, tried to get people calmed down. They reminded everyone about the agreement they'd signed to set up a good government, and it was only after the passengers stopped arguing that we were allowed to get off the ship—which by then, we all hated—and take our first steps on American soil.

Felix and I joined in as everyone concentrated on building a strong fort. Some natives—whom we called "Indians" just as Columbus had, although we, of course, knew we weren't in India— wandered out of their own villages to stare at us. It was December 21, and already very cold.

It came as no surprise to Felix and me that little notice was taken of Christmas Day. There were some prayers said, but that was the extent of it. Felix and I wished we could give toys to the few children in the group, but we hadn't been able to bring any with us on the voyage and there wasn't time after we landed to make gifts before December 25.

"Next year, though, we'll help these children have a wonderful Christmas," I assured Felix.

The winter was a harsh one. The Saints insisted on wearing rather odd clothing, mostly black with white collars and wide belts. They believed wearing bright colors was a sin. Their cloaks were ragged and did little to keep out the cold. The non-Saints had it a little better, dressing for warmth rather than in the plain styles favored by the Saints. The food brought over on the *Mayflower* soon ran out, and we couldn't expect any other ships arriving from England for quite some time, especially since we'd ended up landing so far from where we'd been expected to settle.

In the spring, the Indians saved the people of Plymouth. They showed their new neighbors how to plant crops, and how to use fish as fertilizer. Eventually, there was enough to eat, and in November 1621 William Bradford, who'd been elected governor, announced there would be a special feast called Thanksgiving to celebrate the group's survival. Quite properly, the Indians were invited to join in. Everyone ate a lot; afterward, in the crude shelter we'd built inside the fort, I told Felix, "This wonderful Thanksgiving is a sure sign that Christmas here in Plymouth will be celebrated joyfully!" Felix and I had spent several months secretly making toys out of wooden sticks, bits of cloth, and lumps of clay. Felix still carved beautifully. We eventually made a doll for every little girl in Plymouth, and marbles or a toy wagon for every little boy.

But we weren't allowed to give these gifts. Right after that first Thanksgiving, Governor Bradford announced Christmas would not be celebrated in Plymouth—ever. Astonished, Felix and I rushed to his tent and demanded to know why.

"To set aside December twenty-fifth would be to admit another day is as important as Sunday, the Sabbath," Bradford droned. He was a boring man both in appearance and speech. "If you two have studied your Scripture, you would realize no one truly knows the date of our Lord's birth. So there must be no celebration on the twenty-fifth, none at all."

"You mean, there can be no presents given?" I asked. "Presents are a happy Christmas tradition, and have been for centuries."

"We have come to America to begin new, more proper traditions," Bradford lectured.

Felix shot me a warning look, but I was angry and said to Bradford, "Saint Nicholas won't like this!"

Bradford looked irritated. "There is no place in Plymouth for that ridiculous myth, either. I think I know my history as well as any man, and I'm sure if the real Saint Nicholas were standing here, he'd completely agree with me."

"I wouldn't be so certain," I growled, and Felix grabbed me and hurried me away before I could say more.

Despite our protests, Bradford banned Christmas. All the Saints accepted his decision. Some of the other settlers didn't. Although they weren't allowed to have a Christmas service, they simply took the day off from work and ran around the fort playing games with their children. Bradford wouldn't permit even this. He told them it wasn't right for them to play while the Saints worked. He took away their hoops and sticks and balls and told them that if they had to celebrate at all, they should do it quietly in their tents and log shelters.

Oh, I was furious. I told Felix we should leave Plymouth at once and never, ever come back. "How dare that man Bradford refuse to let people enjoy Christmas?" I fumed. "I've had enough of these Saints, and of this New World called America. As soon as the first ship finds us, you and I are going back to Europe, where Christmas is properly celebrated!"

"Don't be too impatient," Felix suggested. "Surely someone like you, who's almost fifteen hundred years old, must realize some things take time. This place known as America isn't always going to be ruled by such stiff-necked people."

"They don't want Saint Nicholas and his gifts here," I complained.

Felix smiled. "Why don't we spend a year looking around?" he asked. "You just might find that Saint Nicholas is here already." When I said I didn't understand, he added, "These Saints from England aren't the only European settlers, you know."

I'd quite forgotten.

A few hundred miles to the south of Plymouth, Dutch explorers and traders had begun establishing towns. The Dutch had reputations as hardheaded businesspeople, but they also loved celebrations, especially those involving Christmas. Felix's plan was for us to pack up our few belongings and visit some of these Dutch settlements. I agreed, and when Governor Bradford said he wouldn't give us permission to go, we simply left quietly in the middle of the night. The winter weather was harsh, but as usual Felix and I could travel faster than normal humans. We reached the Dutch trading village of Fort Orange in two days.

These villages didn't have as many rules as Plymouth, and the people were friendlier. A British explorer named Henry Hudson had been hired by the Dutch a few years earlier to sail to America and find good land there for them to colonize. When he reported finding a huge harbor, with a wide river connecting it to wonderful green

"America": The New World

valleys, the Dutch were quick to send over their first ships full of colonists. Unlike the Saints, they weren't looking for religious freedom, but for trading opportunities.

In 1621, the main Dutch settlement was Fort Orange in the northern part of what eventually became the state of New York. The people there welcomed Felix and me. Right away they told us they were sorry we'd just missed their celebration of Christmas, when they'd had great feasts and exchanged presents. A little boy named Hans added that on December 6, Saint Nicholas had brought marbles for him and a hoop for his sister.

"The good Saint Nicholas doesn't forget the little children in America," laughed Hans's father. I smiled; obviously, parents in

Fort Orange had brought Saint Nicholas's spirit with them to America, and provided little gifts to their children when I hadn't been around to do so. Well, come next Saint Nicholas Day, I promised myself the pleasure of giving these children their presents.

Felix was quite proud of himself for bringing us to Fort Orange. We decided to stay for a while. We didn't trap animals for their fur, which was what most of the other men in the settlement did. Instead, Felix made some money with his carving, and I spent my days exploring the hills all around the settlement. The Indians were friendly to me once they understood I didn't mean them any harm. It was a pleasurable, peaceful time. I missed Layla terribly, of course, as well as the rest of my longtime friends, but as soon as they learned Felix and I were in Fort Orange they sent letters on every ship that sailed there from European ports, and Felix and I wrote letters back.

Our letters to Europe were filled with happy news, all about how Saint Nicholas and America—at least the Dutch parts of America—were a perfect match. But the letters Layla, Francis, Arthur, and Attila sent us weren't as pleasant.

Europe was still torn by war. When people weren't fighting armies from other countries, they were fighting among themselves. Arthur in particular warned that England was bound to be split apart by civil war. King Charles was unhappy with his Parliament—the elected leaders who helped him govern the country—so he'd simply told the members of Parliament to go home while he ruled all by himself. The Puritans in England opposed Charles. "Sounds like Plymouth all over again to me," Felix commented.

Layla's advice was that Felix and I should stay in America and continue establishing our mission there. The rest of our group would continue on as best they could in Europe. I was pleased to have more time in America, and reluctant to be away from Layla for so long. But my wife and I apparently had thousands of more years to spend together, so Felix and I remained among the Dutch colonists.

These people were, mostly, a very friendly, happy group, and we enjoyed their company. But they weren't perfect, either. As early as 1619, some Dutch colonists earned their livings by importing African slaves to the colonies, where they were often sold to British settlers.

It was about this same time that Dutch leaders met with some trusting chiefs of Indian tribes and bought from them the island called "Manhattan." It was hardly a fair exchange. The colonists got a large island guarding a wide natural port, and the Indians got a few bags of cheap beads. But they'd never seen anything like these beads and considered them to be treasures. The Dutch were careful to have the Indians mark all sorts of legal documents. By European law, the sale was legal.

As soon as the island was theirs, the Dutch sent word back to Holland that more colonists should sail for America. In 1626 a whole fleet arrived, dozens of ships bringing people of every age and profession. These newcomers made up most of the population of a new village on the southern tip of Manhattan Island. The village was named "New Amsterdam" after the most important city in Holland.

Felix and I were watching on the shore as the ships arrived. The leading vessel was called *Goede Vrowe*, Dutch for "Good Housewife." Like all ships of this time, *Good Housewife* had a carved wooden figurehead nailed to its front, since sailors believed these figureheads would protect them from storms. Usually they were the figures of mermaids or other sailors. But as Felix peered at *Good Housewife*, he suddenly blurted, "Nicholas! Look at that figurehead!"

"It looks rather familiar," I replied. "The face, and the robes that are painted such a bright shade of red. I wonder who it's supposed to be?"

"It's you!" Felix shouted. "These settlers carved a figurehead of Saint Nicholas to safely lead them to the New World! It's a sign, Nicholas, don't you see? Christmas has arrived in America, and it's never, ever going to leave!"

But Christmas had to leave England for a while. Even as the Dutch settlers built a statue of Saint Nicholas in their village of New Amsterdam, the Puritans in Britain began an armed uprising against King Charles I. Led by Oliver Cromwell, they eventually captured Charles and executed him. Just like Saints in Plymouth, those Puritans didn't approve of celebrating Christmas with feasts and gifts. In 1645 they ordered everyone in England to treat Christmas like an ordinary day, and said anyone who tried to celebrate the holiday would be punished.

"People all over England are very unhappy with this law," Arthur wrote. "There have been riots in some cities. Canterbury was the worst. Quite a few people were hurt in the protest there. About ten thousand protestors signed a proclamation that they'd have their holiday back even if it meant they had to have a king again, too. I've decided to close down the London toy factory for a while, since these Puritans don't like toys, either. But don't worry; we're just biding our time. Christmas will return to England."

And it did. In 1660, after more civil war, England had a new king, Charles II. Soon afterward, Christmas was restored.

But as Arthur and Layla both wrote, the holiday there wasn't quite the same. Afraid that the Puritans might come back to power, lots of English families stopped openly celebrating December 25, preferring quiet family dinners to singing carols in the streets. Owners of many British companies had taken advantage of the Puritan law to require their employees to work on Christmas Day. Even after King Charles II took the throne, these owners continued to insist that Christmas be an ordinary working day.

"I think we should go back to England for a while," I told Felix. "Something has to be done to make Christmas there what it used to be. Let's find a few special people among these Dutch settlers in New Amsterdam and teach them the ways of gift-making and gift-giving. Then we can return to Europe and rejoin our friends."

But this plan had to be postponed. England and Holland got into a war, one that raged in Europe and affected their colonies in America. England got the better of it. In 1664, the Dutch colonies of Fort Orange and New Amsterdam had to be surrendered to England. The English renamed both villages. Fort Orange was called Albany and New Amsterdam became New York. Fortunately, the English settlers who arrived along with these new names weren't stern Puritans. They not only allowed the Dutch colonists to continue celebrating Christmas with gifts and feasts, they enjoyed joining in the fun. Holland and England continued their war in Europe, which meant Felix and I couldn't safely take a ship back to London, and fighting still occasionally broke out in America between colonists from those two countries. In 1673, the Dutch even retook New York for a little while, but in 1674 the English won it back for good.

New York grew from a village into a city, one of the three largest in America. The other two were Boston to the north and Philadelphia to the south. Colonists flocked to the New World. The hope of religious freedom and lots of green, fertile land was irresistible to people tired of crowded, war-torn Europe.

Late in the 1600s, two new, wonderful names became part of the New World's vocabulary. In 1697, a minister in Boston named Cotton Mather described all New World settlers as "Americans." And, about the same time, English settlers arriving in New York and Albany and other villages established earlier by Dutch colonists found themselves gladly swept up in the Christmas celebrations that had become traditions there. Because most of these settlers had been born after the Puritans banned Christmas in England, they didn't know any legends about a Christmas gift-giver. Their children were thrilled to learn they might have surprise gifts when they woke up on Christmas morning, and begged the Dutch children to tell them all about it.

Since the British now ruled what had been Dutch colonies, English became the official language there and the Dutch had to learn to speak it. This wasn't easy. They had trouble pronouncing certain words in the new language. So when they earnestly began to tell the Christmas stories to their newly arrived English neighbors, they couldn't quite say "Saint Nicholas" clearly. What the English listeners heard was "Sintnicklus" and walked away thinking the gift-giver was "Sinta Klass," which they soon pronounced in a more traditional English way.

For the first time in America, some children began believing that their Christmas presents were delivered by "Santa Claus."

"Oh, really?" General Washington asked again, now leaning so far forward
it appeared he might fall out of the chair onto his face. "They'll
spend all Christmas night singing, and drinking, too?"

EIGHTEEN

Reunion in America

 knock on the door of our log cabin woke Felix and me up from a sound sleep. It was a cool spring night in the thriving village of New York. We'd spent most of the day making toys and had gone to bed feeling very tired.

"I hope it's not another fire," Felix muttered. There had been several blazes in the past months. As New York grew, so did the number of careless people living in it who didn't put out their fires properly before turning in for the night.

Still half-asleep, I stumbled to the door and opened it. Layla rushed in and was hugging me before I realized it. Thrilled to be with my wife again, I hugged Layla back enthusiastically while Felix jumped up to welcome Willie Skokan and Leonardo da Vinci, who came into the cabin behind her.

"Whatever are you doing here?" I asked. "We're happy to see

you, of course, but I thought the plan was for Felix and me to train some new helpers here in America and then rejoin you in Europe."

"You weren't the only one eager to see America," Layla replied briskly, taking off her scarf and not looking a bit older, even though I hadn't seen her for eighty years. "Francis, Attila, and Dorothea have everything in Europe under control, and I'm sad to say that Arthur needs very little help right now in England, since they're still not openly celebrating Christmas there. We decided that it's time to spend the holiday in this country, and we didn't want you and Felix to have all the fun of doing it."

"A new land means a need for new toys," Leonardo added. "Willie Skokan and I want new challenges."

"It would be challenging to fix up these walls a little bit," Willie muttered, feeling along the edges of the logs with his callused fingertips. "Who built this cabin, anyway? There are gaps between the logs."

"Thank you for the compliment, Willie," Felix laughed as he bustled about getting drinks and food for everyone. "Santa and I have been busy learning about this country and making gifts for the many children who are growing up here. We haven't had time for little things like making our own home very comfortable."

"What did you call my husband?" Layla asked, tilting her head to the side as she sometimes did when she heard something that surprised her.

"Santa," Felix answered. "We've told you in our letters about the *Sinta Klass* mispronunciation, and how some children around New York expect Santa Claus to bring their presents. It's a good nickname for Nicholas, don't you think?"

"Santa," Layla repeated thoughtfully. "Yes, it really suits him. I suppose we all ought to call him that from now on."

The five of us spent the rest of the hours before dawn chatting excitedly, catching up on each other's news and making plans for further adventures in America. Felix and I astonished Layla, Leonardo, and Willie Skokan by serving them hot cocoa, a new drink that had become very popular in America but wasn't yet common in Europe. They smacked their lips, enjoying the chocolate taste. When we also served fresh bread with homemade blackberry jam, Leonardo sighed with pleasure.

"Does everyone in America eat so well?" he asked. "When Nicholas—excuse me, when Santa—gives his gifts all over the colonies, do children leave him delicious snacks as they've started to do in Europe?"

"Actually, we haven't had much chance to find out," I admitted. "Because the English now control the colonies along the coast, those unhappy Puritan traditions still are common almost everywhere. Except for New York and Albany and other areas where Dutch Christmas celebrations took hold, December twenty-fifth is almost as poorly celebrated in America as it is in England."

"We think that's just because most of the American colonists haven't heard about Santa Claus yet," Felix chimed in. "Give us a century or two to recruit the right helpers, and every American will look forward to December twenty-fifth. And with three of you here to help us now, it can happen that much sooner!"

The five of us had good intentions, but other events prevented us from accomplishing much in the next few decades.

The American colonies had grown, both in territory and population. By 1700 there were 275,000 settlers. New York had five thousand residents; six thousand people lived in Philadelphia, and seven thousand in Boston. In the next few years, the first American newspapers were published. Farther to the west and south, French-

Canadian trappers founded New Orleans and Spanish missionaries built San Antonio. All over the American continent, men and women with ambition and energy wanted to create their own great nations.

But the nations where they had come from weren't eager for these new Americans to become too independent. England, in particular, which had by far the most colonists, also had the strongest interest in keeping them under control. In the 1740s the first great cotton mills were built in England, but American colonists were forbidden to build their own mills. This meant they would have to buy their cotton cloth from England. Next, the English government told its American colonists that they couldn't settle anywhere west of the Allegheny Mountains, because if settlements were too far inland it would be hard for British soldiers to be stationed there.

Naturally, the colonists felt resentful. They became even angrier when, in 1754, England and France became embroiled in a war over boundaries between each other's American colonies. While the French government cleverly recruited Indians to fight on their side, the English ordered their colonists to enlist and go to war. A lot of them didn't want to fight and were forced into battle. During this nine-year war, a young Virginian named George Washington was made an officer for the English. In fact, he fought in the very first battle of what became known as the French and Indian War.

As usual, we found our powers weakened by being near the fighting. Leonardo and Willie Skokan spent most of their time making gifts, while Felix, Layla, and I began to travel around in hopes of meeting people who could become new helpers. And, of course, all five of us enjoyed those special nights when we delivered our gifts; December 6 in a few communities, December 25 in others, and, for a few years, New Year's Eve and New Year's Day in some Dutch settlements. It so happened that, for whatever reasons, their children hoped for gifts on those two new dates, and, since it made them happy, we were pleased to oblige. After only a hundred years or so, though, almost all children in America wanted their stockings filled when they woke up on Christmas morning.

We recruited our first American helper in 1727. Sarah Kemble Knight was a schoolteacher who wrote the first book about traveling around the country. It was called *A Private Journal of a Journey from Boston to New York in the Year 1704.* That doesn't sound like much of a trip now, but in those days it was a journey that took the better part of two weeks, and required stagecoaches and canoes. Sarah filled her book with comments about the towns she passed through, and the customs of the people who lived in them. Layla happened to meet Sarah in New York in 1726. Over several weeks she explained our mission, and a year later Sarah left her old life behind and joined us. She was wonderfully helpful. It was a great advantage to have someone with us who knew so much about the country and its people.

Sarah Kemble Knight

In 1768 we added another member to our group, though not as a full member who knew all our secrets. Daniel Boone was the first great explorer who had been born to settlers in the colonies. Daniel—he and everyone else really pronounced his name "Dan'l," so that's what I'll call him for the rest of this story—had a restless spirit that reminded me very much of Francis, although Francis was well educated and Dan'l could just read and write simple sentences.

Felix ended up traveling with Dan'l for several years. In 1769 they began to explore the mountain country west of what would be known as North Carolina, and in March 1775, Dan'l led the first settlers along the instantly famous "Wilderness Road" that curved through mountain passes to the rich grasslands of Kentucky. Felix left him there to return to us in New York. When Felix came back, he reported that there seemed no end to how far the American continent stretched toward the western horizon. Someday, Felix predicted, we would need many more helpers to deliver hundreds of thousands of gifts to American children.

"I've asked Dan'l to keep in touch with us so we'll know where new settlements are when we've got enough helpers to deliver presents there," Felix said excitedly. "As soon as this current war business is over with, we can help all Americans learn how to celebrate Christmas properly!"

But what Felix called "this current business" wasn't going to be over as soon as we wished.

For several years, it had been obvious that the American colonists wanted to break away from English rule. In 1774, the group calling itself the First Continental Congress met in Philadelphia. This group, made up of elected representatives from each colony, voted for Americans to stop buying all goods shipped to their country from England. The English weren't pleased. They sent more soldiers to America and, in April 1775, tried to seize a warehouse full of ammunition in Concord, a village in Massachusetts. A silversmith named Paul Revere and several others made frantic, nighttime horseback rides to warn people living in and around Concord that the British were coming. On April 19, 1775, the first shots of the American Revolution were fired.

It turned out to be a very long war, with fighting continuing until 1781. Things were not really over until a peace treaty was signed by the Americans, English, French, and Spanish in 1783. The English armies had better weapons and usually beat the colonists when both armies stopped and faced each other, but the Americans were smart enough not to get into too many battles. Instead, George Washington, picked by the Continental Congress to lead the colonists, kept his soldiers moving continually and attacked the English when they weren't expecting it.

I always hated wars, and I didn't care much for this one. It seemed to me that negotiation would have been better than shooting. But the Revolution was under way, and we in America were in the thick of it. When New York came under attack from the English army, we decided to move south to Philadelphia for a while.

As soon as we arrived in Philadelphia, Leonardo and Willie Skokan told me they wanted to meet a man they'd heard about who was a great inventor.

"This fellow once flew a kite in a thunderstorm to find out more about electricity," Leonardo explained.

"That sounds less like an inventor than an imbecile to me," I replied. "What does a thunderstorm have to do with electricity?"

Willie and Leonardo launched into a long, complicated explanation that just confused me more. People had known about electricity for centuries. It had been William Gilbert, the physician of Henry VIII's daughter Queen Elizabeth, who gave electricity its name. Leonardo even suggested that someday normal people would be able to use electricity in their homes, but for purposes he couldn't yet predict.

Leonardo and Willie Skokan told me that this Benjamin Franklin of Philadelphia thought there might be electricity in lightning, so he went out in a thunderstorm with a metal key attached to the tail of a kite to see if lightning would strike the key and produce electricity.

They also talked about Franklin's printing company, and how every year he'd publish a book called *Poor Richard's Almanack*, which was full of useful information about weather and other things.

Meeting Benjamin Franklin sounded like a more productive way to spend time than worrying about the war. After learning his address, we all went to his home and introduced ourselves. Franklin invited us in, offered us food, and almost immediately fell into deep conversation with Leonardo and Willie Skokan about, of all things, eyeglasses.

"Some people need one type of lens for help with seeing things that are far away, and others need help to see objects that are near," Franklin said.

Benjamin Franklin

"But often when people get older, they need both kinds of eyeglasses and can only wear one at a time. But I have an idea . . ." The three of them disappeared into some side room Franklin used as his laboratory, leaving Felix, Layla, and me behind.

Within two weeks, they'd invented a type of eyeglasses they called "bifocals," with each lens half convex and half concave. And within two months, Benjamin Franklin was a full member of our group.

"I'll have to postpone most of my involvement with you until this war is concluded," he told us. "I'm spending much of my time in France, trying to gain our new nation more support there. Christmas is wonderful, but independence is necessary."

Ben—this is what he told us to call him—understood our dislike of war, and never asked us to help with the Revolution. That December we did help the colonists, however, quite by accident.

General George Washington came to Philadelphia during the third week of that month in 1776 to report to the Continental Congress and to visit his good friend Ben, who was back home briefly from France and invited us one night to have dinner with his famous guest. George Washington was very tall. Later on I read somewhere that he had wooden teeth, but they certainly looked real to me. Ben naturally didn't tell the general who we really were, simply saying that we were visiting from Europe and knew everything there was to know about Europeans and their customs at Christmas.

"Is that so?" General Washington asked. "I wish I knew more about Europeans and their countries. The English have just brought some German soldiers to help against us. We call these troops 'Hessians,' and by reputation they're very good fighters. They've set up a strong camp at Trenton, which isn't too far from here. My soldiers don't believe they can beat the English troops, let alone these Germans. Most of my army is in the countryside around New York, and I'm afraid the Hessians will attack us there."

"Oh, I don't think they'll do that, at least not until after Christmas," Felix observed.

"Why do you think so?" General Washington asked quickly, leaning forward and looking very interested.

"Why, among all people on Earth, Germans may very well like to celebrate Christmas most!" Felix laughed. "I expect the forest around Trenton to be quickly stripped of its evergreen trees, for instance. Your Hessian foes will want to take those trees indoors and decorate them with ribbons and fruit and even candles. Then, on Christmas, I have no doubt they'll gather around those trees all day to sing Christmas carols and drink hot rum."

"Oh, really?" General Washington asked again, now leaning so far forward it appeared he might fall out of the chair onto his face. "They'll spend all Christmas night singing, and drinking, too?"

I suddenly felt uncomfortable with the way the conversation was going. "Perhaps we should change the subject, Felix," I said quickly, but my old friend was already saying more.

"You can count on it, General," Felix babbled cheerfully. "Go back to your troops in New York and tell them they can spend a peaceful Christmas, too."

One week later, on the night of December 25, the Hessian troops in Trenton gathered in their barracks. They stood around Christmas trees and sang carols and drank rum, just as Felix had predicted. And while they did, George Washington and his troops stealthily crossed the Delaware River and surrounded the Hessian camp. On the morning of December 26, while the Hessians were just waking up after their night of celebrating and drinking, Washington's army attacked and overwhelmed them. It was the first major military victory for the colonists, and because of that battle the colonial troops began to believe they could defeat their powerful opponents after all.

Nearly five years later at Yorktown, General Cornwallis of England surrendered to George Washington. Cornwallis said, both then and later, that Washington's Christmas victory over the Hessians was the most important battle in the Revolutionary War, and the moment when the Colonists began to win.

"Well, Felix, it seems you gave George Washington the best Christmas present possible," Ben laughed soon after Cornwallis had surrendered and the war was over. "What a helpful fellow you are."

"Too helpful," I grumbled. We were all crammed into the laboratory at Ben's house. He, Leonardo, and Willie Skokan were hard at work trying to copy a new toy called "roller skates" that had been invented by a helper of Arthur's in London. Apparently, this toy involved putting wheels on the soles of shoes.

"Well," Felix said, "at least the war is over. Now everyone in America can finally learn about Christmas."

We agreed with him that the story was wonderful, but explained what we really wanted him to write was only the part about how Dutch colonists had welcomed Saint Nicholas to help them celebrate Christmas.

NINETEEN

Diedrich Knickerbocker and "Silent Night"

ewly independent America was, in most ways, an exciting place to be. We certainly enjoyed being able to travel up and down its Atlantic coast without worrying about the British army. Sarah Kemble Knight and Ben Franklin were wonderful guides. Layla, Felix, Leonardo, Willie Skokan, and I learned a great deal from them.

The problem we now faced was simple. Except for areas of New York and Pennsylvania where Dutch colonists had settled, Christmas celebrations in America were still inhibited by old-fashioned Puritan influence. In Boston, for instance, people still had to work on December 25, unless that date happened to fall on a Sunday. Each year after the Revolutionary War ended, we could and did choose areas where, on Christmas Eve, we'd quietly enter homes and leave gifts for children to find on Christmas morning. The children would wake up and be delighted with their presents, but they had no idea who had left them. Often their parents were more concerned that someone had come into their homes uninvited, and the next Christmas Eve might even sit up on guard to keep anyone from getting in again. And, as always, if parents didn't want us to come, we felt we shouldn't.

"What we need is some good publicity," Ben Franklin suggested one day in 1808. "You know—stories about Santa Claus and his helpers, and how their gifts can be such a pleasant part of celebrating Christmas."

"Do you mean stories in the newspapers?" Layla asked nervously. There were now quite a few newspapers in America, but none were especially known for telling the truth. "Do you mean we should go to reporters and tell them who we are? I don't think that's a good idea at all."

"She's right, Ben," Leonardo agreed. "If too many people knew our secrets, we'd lose the sense of wonder and magic that makes Santa Claus so special."

It took Sarah, herself an author, to come up with the best solution. "There are several writers in America whose articles and stories are especially well written," she said. "Perhaps we could choose just one writer, someone who could capture Santa's legend on the printed page so that it would inspire everyone's imagination. This way we'd only be sharing our secrets with one person, but that writer could tell our story to parents and children all over America!"

We all thought Sarah's idea was wonderful, and began talking about various American authors whose works we had read and enjoyed. It was Ben, who perhaps read the most of any of us, who insisted he had just the right author in mind.

"There's a fellow in New York named Washington Irving," Ben

suggested. "He's an odd sort, by all accounts, someone who hated school, but then studied law for six whole years because he found the subject interesting. Irving has written several excellent short stories in newspapers about New York and the colonists who came to live there. Let's go meet him and see if he might be interested in helping us."

We found Washington Irving to be a fascinating man. He was short, slender, and balding prematurely at age twenty-six. To arrange our first meeting, we left a note for Irving at his home saying two men who knew all about the early Dutch colonies in Fort Orange and New Amsterdam wanted to talk with him. And this, of course, was true—although it had been almost two hundred years since Felix and I had first lived in them. Still, we both remembered those villages well.

Irving invited us for tea, and didn't seem surprised when seven strangers showed up instead of the two he was expecting. Ben made a good first impression by praising some of Irving's stories that he'd read.

"Right now, most of my new stories are appearing in a newspaper called *Salmagundi*," Irving explained. "I'm not paid very much for writing them. I make most of my money working as a lawyer. I'd rather write. It's my hope one day to spend all my time writing books."

"Why not write a book about the early Dutch colonists?" Ben suggested cheerfully. "I imagine lots of Americans would want to buy such a book to learn more about their customs."

"And their Christmas traditions," Felix added helpfully.

"Do you mean that Saint Nicholas nonsense?" Irving laughed. "I don't think there's anyone left alive who's really certain where that tall tale came from."

"Think again," I replied, and for the next few hours Irving's eyes grew ever wider as he heard the true story of Santa Claus all the way back to when plain old Nicholas first became bishop of Myra. It was especially hard for Irving to believe he was sitting in the same room with Leonardo da Vinci and Benjamin Franklin, but when he was finally convinced he began to chatter frantically.

"I must write this story," he chattered. "I must, I must. What a wonderful tale, Saint Nicholas living forever and coming to America!"

We agreed with him that the story was wonderful, but explained what we really wanted him to write was only the part about how Dutch colonists had welcomed Saint Nicholas to help them celebrate Christmas.

"Why not do what Ben suggested and write a book all about the Dutch colonists," I said. "Let Saint Nicholas be a part of the book. Use that name instead of Santa Claus, the way the Dutch did. This way, everyone who reads it can ease into the whole idea of Santa Claus."

Irving agreed, and for the next six months we stayed with him at his house while he wrote steadily. Irving worried he'd have to work as a lawyer during the day and only write at night, but we arranged for Francis to send us money from Europe, which made up for the salary Irving lost because he wasn't practicing law.

Washington Irving was a great writer, and eventually he would achieve his dream of writing books that were both famous and best-sellers. The book he wrote with us, which was called *Diedrich Knickerbocker's 'A History of New York from the Beginning of the World to the End of the Dutch Dynasty,'* sold quite well by the standards of that time—several thousand copies. You must remember that many Americans still couldn't read in the early 1800s. Irving wouldn't let us read the book while he was writing it. He'd sit in his study, scratching words on paper with his goose-quill pen, and we'd amuse ourselves playing croquet in his yard. Sometimes he'd call us in to give him extra information on one subject or another. Eventually, Irving pronounced the book completed, and he took his hundreds of pages to a printer. Only after the book was bound between covers and displayed for sale in shops would Irving let us read it.

Mostly, we were pleased. Irving wrote of Christmastime in the old Dutch colonies and how "the good Saint Nicholas came riding," with the purpose of bringing "his yearly presents to children." This was good. What wasn't as pleasant was Irving's made-up description of how Saint Nicholas did this by "riding over the tops of trees" in a wagon.

"I can't fly," I spluttered to Irving the first time I read that description. "Why did you say that I could?"

"It seemed to make the story better," Irving replied. "You told me you wanted readers to be thrilled by your Christmas magic."

"Well, my magic doesn't include flying," I grumbled. "I hope everyone who reads your book skips over that part and concentrates on my gift-giving instead."

But when *Diedrich Knickerbocker* was published in 1809, at first it didn't seem as though I'd have much to worry about. As I said, a few thousand copies were sold, and we were able to go into that many more homes on Christmas Eve and leave presents for American children to find on Christmas morning. It was a good start. Then someone who read it was inspired to write a children's book entitled *A New Year's Present to the Little Ones from Five to Twelve,* and in this book I was supposed to ride in a sleigh pulled by a reindeer.

We thanked Irving for his trouble and wished him future success. Though we invited him, he didn't want to leave his home and travel with us. "Writing is my life's purpose, the same way giving gifts to children is yours," Irving explained.

"We'll see you again, I know," Ben told him as we departed. "Meanwhile, happy times are coming for you. With your talent, you're certain to be a world-famous author, and soon."

"I wish you could stay longer," Irving said. "Maybe I could write another book about Saint Nicholas that might sell even better, if you'd stay and give me more good ideas."

"Don't feel badly," Layla suggested. "I have a feeling that *Diedrich Knickerbocker* is going to give us exactly the help we need, although it might take longer than we expected. Write other books. We all agree with Ben that when we see you again, you'll be famous."

We were sorry to say good-bye to Washington Irving, but excited to be on our way because, after so many years, we had decided to take a ship back to Europe. We wouldn't stay there forever—it was understood among us that America would probably be our permanent home—but we wanted to see Arthur and Francis and Attila and Dorothea again. Sarah, Felix, and Ben Franklin stayed behind to open up a toy factory in Philadelphia and keep building the American Christmas tradition until the rest of us returned.

In the spring of 1810 we sailed back to London. Arthur met us at the dock. Francis was with him, and so were Attila and Dorothea, who'd come all the way from Nuremberg to greet us. That night we had a wonderful reunion dinner at Arthur's home, and heard about the latest news in Britain.

"You might have left America just in time," Arthur suggested. "Everyone here in England believes we'll soon be at war with the colonists again."

"They're not 'colonists' anymore, Arthur," Layla said gently. "They want to be called Americans now."

"Whatever they call themselves, I think they were lucky to defeat the British," Arthur snorted. "If I didn't know better, I'd think that General Washington had some sort of special help. None of you would know anything about that, would you?" We all shook our heads and did our very best to look innocent.

But Arthur was right about another war between America and Britain. The two countries got in a fierce argument over shipping rights—whose ships could go where, carrying what—and finally war was declared in 1812. Again, it was fought in America, and mostly the British got the best of it. In May 1814, their army actually burned some of Washington; President James Madison had to run away as part of the White House went up in flames. But four months later an American named Thomas Macdonough won a terrible naval battle on Lake Champlain in New York State, and soon afterward leaders from both sides met in Belgium and signed a peace treaty. They did this on Christmas Eve, saying it was appropriate to stop fighting on Christ's birthday. There was one more battle in this war to be fought, though. News of the peace treaty didn't reach New Orleans before January 8, 1815. Thinking America was still at war, General Andrew Jackson routed his British foes. Thank goodness, this was the last battle ever between America and Britain.

We were still determined to help make Christmas a happier holiday in America, but we also wanted to enjoy a few European Christmases in countries that celebrated the season properly with traditional visits from Saint Nicholas, by whatever name and on whatever date. Leonardo and Willie Skokan happily went right back to work at the Nuremberg toy factory. Layla and I joined Arthur, Attila, and Dorothea on some of their gift-giving adventures, and went out on our own several times, particularly in Italy. How wonderful it was to be among people who held Christmas in their hearts, with carols and Christmas trees and nativity scenes and presents and, most of all, honest, grateful joy for the birth of Jesus that didn't have to be concealed for fear of someone else thinking such happiness was inappropriate.

In 1818, a few years after we'd come back to Europe, Layla asked me if the two of us might spend a special Christmas together. "I love our friends and our gift-giving, Santa," she said, using the American name for me that all of us liked best. "But just once, after all these years, I wonder if we couldn't spend one Christmas Eve quietly, just the two of us, going somewhere special and celebrating at a midnight church service just as normal people do?"

In all our years together, this was the first favor Layla had asked of me. I was more than happy to agree. When we told our friends, they all had suggestions about where we should go for our holiday.

"A second honeymoon for you!" Dorothea laughed. "How wonderful! What fun!"

"We never had a first honeymoon," Layla replied. "We were married in the afternoon, and we helped Felix give gifts that night. It's taken me thirteen centuries to get this husband of mine alone for a while!"

Attila had heard of an Austrian village named Oberndorf, just eleven miles north of the city of Salzburg.

"It's lovely country; the Salzach River runs right beside the town," he said. "Best of all, the villagers there have their midnight worship service in Saint Nicholas's Church! It's named for you!"

Obviously, Layla and I chose to spend our holiday in Oberndorf. We arrived there a few days before Christmas and arranged to stay at a comfortable inn. I hadn't ever had a vacation, and was surprised how pleasant one could be. Layla and I slept late, ate what we pleased, and took long walks along the banks of the river. It was on the last of those walks, during the morning of December 24, that we passed Saint Nicholas's Church and saw a tall man wearing a priest's robes standing outside talking with a stocky fellow. They were obviously upset, although not with each other.

"Pardon us, gentlemen," I said as Layla and I approached them. "We don't wish to interrupt, but tonight we plan to attend Christmas mass and wonder when the service will begin."

"There might not be a midnight service, or, at least, there might not be a very special one," the heavyset man mumbled. "Christmas mass without music won't seem like Christmas at all."

"We can't give up so easily, Franz," the priest said. He smiled at Layla and me and added, "I'm Father Josef Mohr, assistant priest of this church, and this is Franz Gruber, our church organist. We pride ourselves on our Christmas midnight mass, especially since our church is named for the saint who many believe is the example of true holiday spirit. People come from all over to celebrate Christmas with us, but we've just discovered our church organ is somehow not working. Franz thinks mice have been nibbling too much at the pedals, and I believe mist from the river must have damaged the pipes."

"It doesn't matter what's wrong with the organ, Father," Franz said unhappily. "It won't play and there's no time to have it repaired before tonight's service. Christmas without music just isn't Christmas, as I said before."

"Can't everyone just sing without music?" Layla asked.

"The organ music is necessary for all the traditional carols," Franz brooded. "Tonight's mass will be a disappointment to everyone. Well, I'll go back inside and work on the organ some more. Maybe Saint Nicholas himself will arrive tonight with a new organ so we can have music after all."

"Don't think badly of Franz," Father Mohr cautioned after the organist disappeared into the church. "It's just that he loves music so much, and loves Christmas so much, too. We can still have a happy service without music. We'll celebrate the birth of Jesus with songs in our hearts and not on our lips, I suppose."

Father Mohr seemed very agreeable. Layla and I invited him to eat lunch with us. Afterward, he invited us back to the church and showed us all around. There was a beautiful stained-glass window of Saint Nicholas in his old-fashioned red bishop's robes trimmed with white.

"Quite a handsome fellow," I said.

"A thin fellow, too," Layla whispered rudely. I chose dignified silence as my best response.

Because it was winter, darkness came early to Oberndorf. Although it was cold, the air felt crisp and the sky was clear. Layla, Father Mohr, and I stood outside the church looking up at the stars. In the village, families were inside their homes getting ready for dinner. Afterward, they'd walk to the church for midnight mass. Then there would be much bustling in the streets, and loudly shouted wishes to each other of "Merry Christmas." But for now, everything was blissfully silent.

"This is such a silent night," Layla mused. "And somehow it feels like a holy night, as well."

Father Mohr's brow furrowed. He pulled a stick of charcoal and a scrap of paper from his pocket and began scribbling. "Did you say this is a silent night, a holy night?" he asked Layla.

"Yes," she replied, looking puzzled.

"Come with me—hurry!" Father Mohr blurted, turning and running into the church. "Franz Gruber! Franz Gruber! Come here quickly, and bring your guitar!"

Three hours later, and just minutes before the first worshipers arrived at Saint Nicholas's Church, Father Josef Mohr and Franz

Gruber had written a new Christmas carol. It began with Layla's words: "Silent night, holy night." Using simple, heartfelt rhyme, Father Mohr had continued, "All is calm. All is bright." From there, he let his song with its lovely melody and plain words tell the story of the night of Jesus' birth.

Just after midnight on December 25, 1818, the climax of mass at Saint Nicholas's Church in Oberndorf came when Father Mohr and Franz Gruber stood before the congregation. Father Mohr held a sheet of paper in his hands, with words and musical notes written on it. He held the paper in front of Franz Gruber, who strummed his guitar. Father Mohr sang tenor. Franz Gruber sang bass. As their listeners sat transfixed, they sang:

> *Silent night, holy night.*
> *All is calm. All is bright.*
> *'Round yon virgin mother and child.*

As they continued to sing, many men and women in the church began to weep with joy. Tears running down their faces, they begged to hear the song again, and again. By the fourth time Father Mohr and Franz Gruber sang, the entire congregation was standing and singing with them. Standing with my wife, Layla, singing and crying at the same time like everyone else, I somehow knew, *knew,* that our voices were carrying up through the roof of the church, through the cold Christmas night air, all the way up to Heaven, where the one whose birth we were singing about was listening and smiling, pleased with the love and joy reflected in this new, incredible carol.

After the service, the villagers of Oberndorf walked quietly home, as though speaking might somehow break a special spell. There was no need for Layla and me to hurry away from the church. We knew

Attila and Dorothea and their helpers had delivered presents to the children of Oberndorf and all of Austria on December 6, Saint Nicholas Day.

"Thank you," Layla said softly to Father Mohr.

"Thank you," he replied. We took turns hugging him, and then Layla and I, too, returned to the village. I looked back once and saw Father Mohr staring up at the dark Christmas sky. Abruptly, he raised his hand toward the stars, waving to the Savior he'd just celebrated in a song that would be part of Christmas forever.

We left Oberndorf the next day, feeling especially joyful, and returned to Nuremberg, where we happily rejoined our friends and continued our gift-giving work. Then one morning, five years later, Attila told me he'd received a message from Arthur, who wanted Layla and me to return to London as soon as possible.

"Has someone been hurt?" I asked worriedly. "Has there been an accident at Arthur's toy factory?"

"The message said it was nothing bad, but still a matter that required you to come right away," Attila said. Layla, Leonardo, Willie Skokan, and I left immediately, traveling as quickly as we could, which was ten times faster than ordinary mortals.

When we reached London, we hurried to the toy factory and burst into Arthur's office. "What's happened?" I asked.

Arthur raised an eyebrow; in reply, he handed me a letter in Felix's handwriting.

It said simply, "Come back to America at once. Everyone knows about you now. You're famous."

There was also a mysterious postscript: "Please bring flying reindeer. Eight, if possible."

"Simply shout out, 'Now, Dasher, now, Dancer, now, Prancer and Vixen; on, Comet, on Cupid, on, Donder and Blitzen!' Then they'll run and the sleigh will take off."

TWENTY

Reindeer Fly,
and So Do I

 mong those who had read *Diedrich Knickerbocker,* Washington Irving's book that included the Dutch colonists' belief in Saint Nicholas, was Clement Moore, well known in New York as a great scholar and historian. Moore loved Irving's book, and his favorite passages were about the long-lived saint who gave Christmas presents to children.

In 1822, Moore invited several relatives to join him and his family for Christmas. Moore's favorite daughter, Charity, begged him to write a poem for the occasion, because her father often wrote verses for special family gatherings.

Now, Clement Moore was a busy man. For a while he forgot about his promise to Charity. On December 23, relatives began arriving for the Christmas celebration, and that afternoon Mrs. Moore asked her husband to go to the market and buy some food they needed for that evening's meal. It was a snowy day, and Moore made the trip in a horse-drawn sleigh. He had allowed his daughter Charity to come with him, and on their ride home she asked if he'd written his special Christmas poem yet.

"I didn't want to disappoint my little girl," Moore told us nearly ten years later, when we'd become his friends and often joined him for long evening talks. "When we got home, I went upstairs to my study and closed the door. I remembered reading *Diedrich Knicker-bocker*, and took the book down from a shelf. Washington Irving is such a wonderful writer! I loved his descriptions of Saint Nicholas, especially when the saint would place his finger beside his nose and fly away."

Moore also referred to another small book, titled *The Children's Friend*. That one included a sketch of Saint Nicholas driving a sleigh pulled by reindeer.

"An idea for a poem began to form in my mind," Moore said. "All my children loved the Christmas holiday, after all, and we'd always kept the tradition of having presents for the children to open on Christmas morning. From the history I'd studied, I'd long suspected Saint Nicholas really did exist, and that he somehow was able to bring gifts to children during the holidays. So I was determined to write my poem about him, and include all the wonderful stories from the Dutch colonists. My remaining problem was describing what he looked like, for I wanted my children and family to be able to per-fectly picture him in their minds as they listened to my poem."

As it happened, the Moore family employed a gardener named Jan Duyckinck. He was of Dutch descent, white-bearded and some-what overweight. Also, Jan was a jolly fellow who always did his work cheerfully, and with a small pipe clenched between his teeth.

"When I thought of Jan, the whole poem seemed to come into

my head at once," Moore concluded. "I wrote for several hours. Then, after dinner on that night of December twenty-third, 1822, I called everyone into the parlor and began to read to them."

Every line, every word, was to become famous. Moore titled his poem "A Visit from Saint Nicholas." It began:

'Twas the night before Christmas, and all through the house
Not a creature was stirring, not even a mouse.

It was a short poem, fifty-six lines in all. When Moore completed his recitation, everyone clapped and cheered. He was pleased by his family's response and thought that one reading was the last anyone would ever hear of "A Visit from Saint Nicholas."

But someone among Moore's listeners that night—he never found out who—considered the poem too good to be forgotten. This person secretly copied the poem and gave it to the editor of the *Troy Sentinel,* a newspaper in a nearby town. The editor obviously loved the poem, too, because exactly one year later, on December 23, 1823, "A Visit from Saint Nicholas" was published in the *Sentinel* and became an immediate sensation. Every copy of that day's newspaper was sold. Newspapers and magazines all over the rest of America reprinted the poem in its entirety. It seemed every American parent who read the poem immediately decided to make Saint Nicholas welcome, and all the children who heard the now-famous lines went to bed on Christmas Eve with visions of sugarplums dancing in their heads, and in hopes that Saint Nicholas soon would arrive to leave them presents.

There were two other important, immediate reactions. Felix, Sarah, and Ben Franklin, my poor helpers who had stayed behind in America, were suddenly overwhelmed by the number of homes in which they were welcome, and in which they were now expected to leave gifts on Christmas Eve. They worked frantically to satisfy as many eager children as possible. And Clement Moore, who considered himself a serious scholar, felt embarrassed by the attention being given to something he thought of as an enjoyable but still silly little poem. The *Troy Sentinel* hadn't printed the name of the poet, and for many years Moore tried to keep his identity a secret.

Felix and the others thought the sensation caused by the poem might die down after a year or so, but instead the popularity of "A Visit from Saint Nicholas" spread. Children now believed they knew all about me from that poem. By 1825, Felix felt he had no choice but to summon me back to America from Europe, and sent his urgent message to Arthur.

Layla, Leonardo, Willie Skokan, and I were able to get back quickly. The first steamship had crossed the Atlantic Ocean in 1819, and this new method of sea transportation cut sailing time between England and America in half. Felix, Sarah, and Ben met us at the dock.

"Whatever did you mean, 'Bring flying reindeer. Eight, if possible'?" I asked Felix as soon as my feet touched land.

"You'll understand soon," he assured me, and within hours we new arrivals were sitting comfortably in the house Felix and the others had built in New York, reading "A Visit from Saint Nicholas" for ourselves.

I very much enjoyed the first dozen lines or so. "This is simply wonderful!" I chortled, but Layla, who read faster, suggested I save my rapturous comments until I'd read further. And when I got to the lines describing what the father saw as he "tore open the shutters and drew up the sash," I began to choke. Everyone jumped up to pound me on the back.

"I can't believe this," I bellowed. "Reindeer pulling my sleigh through the sky? Eight reindeer? Reindeer with names, for goodness sakes! Why, this fellow has me landing on a roof!"

Most of the rest of the poem was acceptable, even pleasing—the part about filling the stockings was my favorite—but I didn't feel I could overlook Moore's rude comments about my weight.

"He says I've got a little round belly," I complained.

"Well, actually, you've got rather a big round belly," Willie Skokan observed, meaning, I suppose, to be helpful. Everyone enjoyed a good laugh at my expense before Felix added carefully, "You might also note the forty-sixth line."

I reread it and gasped with horror. "Why, I'm not an elf! I'm a full-grown man, and don't you say what I know you're thinking, Layla!" My wife had opened her mouth to make a sarcastic remark, but now she closed it again. "This poem is going to cause us problems, my friends. Now, I'm glad it was written, and gladder still it's become beloved and made Americans want us to be part of their Christmas holiday. But it's always been our rule to become whatever children of each country expect us to be, and in this case it may be impossible. I'm not an elf, for one thing, and can't become one to satisfy the expectations created by this poem."

"I really don't think the children will care if you're an elf or not," Layla commented. "That can be like the myth of you coming down chimneys, part of the illusion but not really vital to the real mission, which is delivering the toys. It's the flying-reindeer issue that we have to deal with."

"We actually have gone down a few chimneys if the chimneys were wide enough and if there was no other easy way to get into a house," Felix noted. "The problem here in America, as I see it, is that countless children will be peering out windows every Christmas

Eve, hoping for a glimpse of Saint Nicholas and his sleigh flying through the night sky."

"Let me just correct you by noting many American children, perhaps the majority of them, use the name 'Santa Claus' instead of 'Saint Nicholas,' " Sarah interrupted. "On my last trip along the coast I learned this. I wish Clement Moore had chosen to write 'A Visit from Santa Claus' to avoid future confusion, but I assume he was trying to remain faithful to the Dutch traditions, and—"

"I don't mean to be rude, but can we please concentrate on the flying reindeer?" I asked impatiently. "Everything else can be worked out, but we have a simple problem that can't be ignored. Reindeer cannot fly."

"I think they can," Leonardo said in a soft but assured voice. "That is, I think they can under the correct circumstances and with the proper equipment."

Leonardo, Ben, and Willie Skokan were sitting together by the front of the fireplace, and I saw that they had one of Leonardo's notebooks in front of them. As usual, its pages were full of diagrams and mathematical formulas.

"I don't think reindeer can sprout wings, Leonardo," I said as patiently as possible. "Do you know of a herd that has?"

Leonardo was a very serious person. I don't think he realized I was being sarcastic. "No, Santa, but wings on the reindeer themselves might not be necessary for flight. I've been pondering the possibility of flight for the better part of three centuries now, and I'm convinced that flying is a matter of speed and air mass. Look at these sketches in my notebook." He handed me the notebook, but I hadn't the slightest idea of what the diagrams I was looking at might mean.

Before I could say anything more that might have hurt Leonardo's feelings, Ben interjected, "Willie Skokan and I are convinced there must be a way reindeer can fly, too. Of course, it's not really a matter of the reindeer flying so much as it's a question of how to put them in a position where they can be attached to the right device that would allow flight."

"Can you say it more simply?" I asked wearily.

"Let us get some reindeer and start working," Ben said. "Leonardo and Willie Skokan and I will find a way reindeer can fly, if only you'll be patient."

"Santa will be patient, Ben, but I wouldn't count on American children doing the same," Layla advised. "Please find some brilliant solution as quickly as you can."

And so Leonardo, Ben, and Willie Skokan set to work. They sailed back across the Atlantic Ocean to Europe, then went north to the remote Scandinavian snows of Lapland. This was where reindeer roamed, handsome animals standing three and one half feet high and weighing about three hundred pounds. Both male and female reindeer have wide, heavy antlers, and heavy hoofs. Fortunately, they can be tamed, though not easily. Some Laplanders used them to pull sleds. My three helpers could have purchased reindeer from Lapland farmers, but they preferred venturing out onto the frozen tundra and capturing their own.

"We wanted only the very best," Ben explained when they finally returned to America after a hard trip home. It had taken them nearly ten months to round up eight reindeer Leonardo considered suitable: great, powerful animals whose eyes shone with intelligence. In anticipation of their arrival, we had purchased property in the far hill country of New York State, near a village called Cooperstown. This property was far enough removed from public gaze that we felt it might be possible for Leonardo to conduct his flying-reindeer experiments in relative privacy.

The reindeer were installed inside a snug barn. The rest of us were given boring daily chores to perform—buying grain for their feed bags, raking out stalls—while Leonardo, Ben, and Willie Skokan would put halters on the reindeer and lead them off into the hills for training they wouldn't describe to the rest of us. Helpers and reindeer never got back until well after dark each night. Sometimes Ben and Willie would be smiling. More often, they'd look tired and frustrated. Leonardo's expression never changed. He always looked thoughtful.

Christmas of 1826 passed, then Christmas of 1827. We gave gifts as best we could, and children all over America peeked out their windows on Christmas Eve, watching in vain for Santa flying by with his reindeer.

"I don't think Leonardo can do it," Felix said sadly as Christmas 1828 approached. "We have to face it: As great as our magic has been, some miracles are beyond us, and flying reindeer happen to be one of them."

"I still have faith in Leonardo," Layla replied.

It was just the next night when the three would-be reindeer trainers came trooping into the house with huge grins on their faces. Even Leonardo looked pleased.

"We need Felix to come with us tomorrow," Ben announced. "He's not as good a carpenter as Willie Skokan, but we'll need his help, if only to carry wood and tools."

"I can come help, too," I said quickly, but Ben shook his head.

"Just Felix, I think," he commanded. "We want you to be surprised."

Felix left with the other three in the morning, and looked tired when he returned with them after dark. His hands were scratched from hard labor. When I asked what kind of work he'd been doing, he shook his head and wouldn't tell me.

"I promised I'd keep the secret," he muttered, and fell asleep in front of the fire soon after supper.

Felix began working with Leonardo, Ben, and Willie Skokan in early October. By mid-November, my curiosity was too great to control.

"Tell me what's going on!" I demanded one night as we all sat around the dinner table. "I can tell by your smiles that even Layla and Sarah are in on the secret. I'm the only one who doesn't know. Tell me now, quickly—will there be flying reindeer this Christmas?"

"Wait and see, Santa," Ben advised.

"I've waited long enough," I grumbled, and everyone else laughed.

One morning three weeks later, I was awakened at dawn by Layla. "Put on your warmest clothing," she ordered. "We're all going out with the reindeer." I quickly dressed and waited impatiently while the others ate breakfast. When they finally finished, we put halters on the reindeer and hiked some two miles to the top of the highest hill on the property, where a large, mysterious object was concealed under an equally huge sheet of canvas.

"Are you ready?" Ben asked me, grinning fiendishly as Willie Skokan and Leonardo took hold of the canvas. "Are you prepared to discover whether reindeer really know how to fly?"

"Enough of this foolishness," I snapped. "I see the reindeer standing right here, and they're no different than they were when you first brought them to America. They surely can't fly, Ben. They have no wings!"

"But they will, and besides, this does, too!" Ben announced, and with a theatrical flourish of his hand gestured for Leonardo and Willie Skokan to reveal what was under the canvas.

I saw a sleigh, but a sleigh unlike any that could ever have existed before. It had the usual wide bed, and a long front pole to which harness could be attached. And extending from the sides of the sleigh, not very far but still sticking out, were what appeared to be curved, shaped wings.

"What does all this mean?" I asked.

Leonardo hurried to my side, brandishing one of his notebooks and pointing to a sketch on one page. "You see, Santa, it's not really the reindeer themselves who fly," he explained. "The reindeer provide the thrust, the power, if you will, to make the wind flow under the wings of the sleigh and also under the smaller wings we've attached to each reindeer's harness. This wind mass under the wings lifts up the reindeer and the sleigh."

"I have no idea what you're talking about," I replied honestly. "Can you or someone else please use words I can understand?"

Ben said, "In the simplest terms, Santa, if the reindeer can pull the sleigh fast enough, it will fly. And these reindeer can do just that. Back in Lapland, we selected the eight fastest reindeer. When they're hitched to the sleigh and begin to run, the wings on the sleigh and the harness cut through the air. Enough air gets under the wings to lift the sleigh and the reindeer, too."

Eager to tell me more, Leonardo added, "We've factored in the weight of a load of toys, and also the weight of a driver, who is meant to be you, Santa. I didn't know how much you weighed, but Layla said she could guess, so I took her word for it."

I swung my gaze over to my wife. "And how much did you say I weighed?"

Layla smiled. "Don't ask. Why not just thank Leonardo for his brilliance, and everyone else for their hard work?"

So I offered my thanks, and suggested we might as well take the sleigh and the reindeer back to the house.

"Wait, Santa," Felix said. "Don't you want to see the reindeer pull the sleigh and fly through the sky?"

"I'm sure you've tested the whole process thoroughly," I answered. "Good for you. Well, let's go home."

"Wait, Santa," Layla said in a tone that made it clear she expected me to do as I was told. "All this work has been done so you can fly this sleigh on Christmas Eve, just a month from now. You must climb aboard the sleigh. Look, Willie Skokan is loading toys on it so the weight will be exactly right. Try it for yourself."

Before I could protest, Ben took one of my arms, Felix took the other, and they propelled me toward the sleigh and onto its seat. There was a belt attached to the seat, and this was secured around my midsection—"So you won't fall off," Felix said alarmingly. Leonardo hitched up the reindeer and handed me the reins.

"They've been very well trained," he assured me. "We have a signal that tells them to start running. It involves their names."

"What names?" I spluttered.

"Why, the names given to them in Clement Moore's poem," Leonardo said innocently. "I assumed you wanted to keep everything as close to that story as possible, so American children won't be disappointed. I'll whisper the command now, so they won't hear me and start too soon. Simply shout out, 'Now, Dasher, now, Dancer, now, Prancer and Vixen; on, Comet, on Cupid, on, Donder and Blitzen!' Then they'll run and the sleigh will take off."

Everyone but Felix backed away, waiting for me to give the reindeer their signal. Even the reindeer themselves seemed pleased at the prospect, as all eight looked back at me with expectant eyes. The small wings on each reindeer's harness seemed to flutter with anticipation. I sat still and didn't make a sound.

Blixen

Felix leaned over and whispered to me. "What's wrong?"

I whispered back, "I can't remember the whole signal."

"That's all right. Just in case, we've also trained them to run when the driver shouts, 'Go!'" Felix assured me.

I still didn't move.

"What's the matter now?" Felix inquired softly.

I told him the truth: "I'm afraid of heights."

"Well, time to get over it," Felix muttered unsympathetically. He stepped back and, to my absolute horror, shouted, "Go!"

The reindeer responded instantly. My arms were nearly tugged from their sockets as the reins tightened and the eight-animal team surged forward. They ran madly over the snow, the sleigh bumping along the ground behind them. For twenty yards, I bumped along, then fifty, and I started thinking Leonardo had been wrong, and then the wind began to whistle and the sleigh took a sudden lurch. I looked in front of the sleigh at the reindeer, and then down, and the ground was well below me. Layla, looking no larger than an ant, was waving. I suspected she was also laughing.

The poor man actually had tears in his eyes as I described the wonders
of English Christmases past. When I finally finished with the
tale of how Washington Irving had suggested I come to London,
Dickens pulled a handkerchief out of his pocket and
blew his nose in a series of loud honks.

TWENTY-ONE

A Christmas Carol

fter I learned to drive a team of flying reindeer properly—and it took me a few years, too, with some very
embarrassing accidents I choose not to describe here—I
made it a point every Christmas Eve to make my last American stop
for the night at Clement Moore's house. The first time I landed on
his lawn—not on the roof, because roofs as a rule are too steep to
make good landing areas for reindeer—I saw him peeking through
his bedroom window curtain. Smiling in spite of myself, I motioned
for him to meet me inside.

We ended up chatting for almost an hour, sitting comfortably in
his parlor beside a huge Christmas tree, and had such a pleasant time
we decided to make a tradition of it. Poor Clement apologized pro-
fusely when I told him what great trouble his description of flying
reindeer had caused me, but I assured him things had turned out

well. In fact, I had even overcome my fear of heights and quite enjoyed soaring through the skies with Dasher and Dancer and the rest of my four-legged friends.

On Christmas Eve 1842, Clement had a surprise for me. I landed on his lawn as usual, tired from my long night's work and looking forward to the delicious chocolate chip cookies Mrs. Moore always baked fresh that afternoon for me. Clement welcomed me inside and, before I could ask for my cookies, said he wanted me to shake hands with someone.

"Don't worry, Santa, I haven't given away your secrets to a stranger," he laughed. "I think you already know this gentleman." We went into the parlor and there, sitting beside the warm fire, was none other than Washington Irving.

"It's wonderful to see you again," I told him by way of greeting. "Your *Diedrich Knickerbocker* made me welcome in America after all, with its influence on Clement's 'A Visit from Saint Nicholas.' "

"Actually, most people have begun to call that poem "Twas the Night Before Christmas' after its first line," Irving corrected. "The original title is well on its way to being forgotten. Still, I'm proud that my book was Clement's inspiration."

Clement bustled about getting us all hot cocoa to drink. As he did, I told Irving, "Congratulations, of course, on all your success as an author. You certainly accomplished your goal of becoming world famous and widely read. What was the name of that one book, the collection of short stories, and the title of that popular story in particular?"

"I think you mean *The Sketch Book of Geoffrey Crayon,*" Irving laughed. "You might remember I was living in England when I wrote that one. And the story in it to which I'm sure you refer is 'The Legend of Sleepy Hollow.' I have to admit I'm surprised it was so popular, what with its references to a headless horseman and so forth. Perhaps it will become closely associated with that so-called holiday of Halloween, the way Clement's poem is eternally linked with Christmas."

The three of us chatted until almost dawn, when I rose to take my leave before Clement's countless children and grandchildren spilled down the stairs to see what presents Santa might have left for them. As I gathered up the handful of sugar lumps Clement always gave me as a parting present for the reindeer, Irving asked me, "Now that you've conquered America, so to speak, what do you want to do next?"

"It continues to trouble me that Christmas is still so poorly celebrated in England," I replied. "My friends, I tell you that once upon a time there was no country that enjoyed happier Christmas holidays. Oliver Cromwell and his henchmen ruined that, and I won't be completely at peace with myself until British Christmases return to their old, joyous heights."

Irving looked thoughtful for a moment, then said, "I received a letter not long ago from an English writer whose work I admire. In it, he said how much he'd enjoyed a short story of mine about a mythical Christmas celebration at the home of a fictional English squire, and how he was determined to restore the tradition of wonderful Christmas holidays in his country. His name is Charles Dickens. He might be of help to you, and you could be of help to him."

Within a month, I'd written to Dickens asking to visit him in London, identifying myself only as someone who shared both his enthusiasm for the Christmas holiday and his desire to again make it a special part of British life. In October, having received a warm and enthusiastic invitation to Dickens's home, Layla and I sailed back to England. We had a happy reunion with Arthur when we docked, and the next morning I strolled across London to meet with Charles Dickens.

Please understand that, except on my holiday gift-giving excursion, whenever I was out in public I wore ordinary clothing so as not to draw attention to myself. My full white beard and somewhat stout stature never seemed to remind anyone I passed of Santa Claus. But the moment Dickens opened his front door and saw me standing on the step, he immediately said, "You're Father Christmas!" Remember, this was the name by which I'd once been widely known in England, and what I was still called by the remaining English children who were allowed to believe in me and expect my Christmas visits.

"Not so loud!" I cautioned. "May I please come in?"

"Of course!" Dickens boomed, and ushered me into a very nice home. "My study is just to the left. Please make yourself comfortable sitting on this chair, not that other, which has seat-spring cushions which sometimes cause discomfort.

"Well, Father Christmas is here in my own home! I knew you really existed, I just knew it! There's been too much joy surrounding the holidays, too much happiness for there not to have been someone special involved for countless centuries! You really must tell me all about it!"

I did, and Dickens sat listening for hours. Sometimes he'd interrupt with questions, but mostly he nodded. The poor man actually had tears in his eyes as I described the wonders of English Christmases past. When I finally finished with the tale of how Washington Irving had suggested I come to London, Dickens pulled his handkerchief out of his pocket and blew his nose in a series of loud honks.

"Father Christmas, please help me find a way to restore proper Christmases to England," he pleaded. "Although I've tried, I'm afraid my own poor talents aren't equal to the task."

"How have you tried?" I wondered.

Dickens frowned, an expression I later learned was usual for him. The man truly had an odd face, pinched around the eyes and dominated by one of the largest noses I'd ever seen. Even Dickens's hair was strange, very thin on top and thick and curly around his ears.

"As you know, I'm a writer," he explained. "By most standards, I'm a rather successful one, too. Some of my novels have sold very well, particularly *Oliver Twist, Nicholas Nickleby,* and *The Pickwick Papers.* But the public likes my books better than it does the other causes I promote, namely better working conditions in the factories and better treatment of the poor. These are hard times for the less fortunate, Father Christmas, and that's a fact. This is why I think it's so important for Christmas to become glorious again, so everyone, young and old, rich and poor alike, can have at least one day of the year where problems and differences are put aside and everyone can celebrate together."

It was an impressive speech; Dickens was out of breath at the end of it. I sat thinking for a few moments, then said, "Have you tried writing stories about Christmas? The right book or poem can work Christmas wonders; in America, Washington Irving's novel and Clement Moore's poem have done that."

Dickens ducked his head, looking ashamed. "I've tried, Father Christmas. Some years ago I published 'A Christmas Dinner,' a short story about how a family sitting down for their holiday meal is able to forgive past arguments and insults."

"A lovely theme," I commented.

"Perhaps, but the story was ignored," Dickens said ruefully. "I then attempted to stir up interest in Christmas by including a holiday tale in *The Pickwick Papers.* I called this story 'The Goblins Who Stole a Sexton,' and in it a cold, unfriendly man who hates the

Christmas happiness of others is taken one night by ghostly beings on adventures which teach him how wonderful Christmas is, after all. Well, *The Pickwick Papers* was widely commented upon, but no one reading it seemed to understand the special Christmas message I meant to convey."

"That certainly is too bad," I said with great sympathy. "You are obviously someone who truly holds Christmas in his heart, and long ago I learned to put my trust in fate. Since we've been brought together, I believe it's meant for us to work on behalf of the holiday. However, I notice it's getting late, and by the toys scattered about your home I perceive you must be a married man with children."

Dickens nodded. "My children are truly the joy of my life, Father Christmas. My wife has taken them today to visit with her parents, and I expect them home momentarily."

"It's best I leave, then," I said, standing up and stretching. "Be careful not to tell your family about my visit or the things I've told you. I always prefer as few people as possible knowing such secrets. Could you, perhaps, lend me copies of your Christmas stories? I'll read them tonight and tomorrow you might call on me, my wife, and our friend Arthur at his toy factory. We can talk more there."

Walking back to Arthur's in the early evening darkness, enjoying the coolness of the crisp late autumn air, I felt pleased to have met Dickens and wondered how to help him. Arthur, Layla, and I sat up most of the night reading his stories, which were truly excellent. We exclaimed over especially well-written scenes and agreed that such a talented writer as Charles Dickens surely could create a story so wonderful, so moving, that everyone reading it would pledge to celebrate Christmas properly forever afterward.

"Do you suppose we should pay to have these stories printed again and distributed all over England?" Arthur asked.

Layla shook her head. "For whatever reason, they have not accomplished their purpose despite being written so well," she reminded him. "My suggestion would be for Mr. Dickens to try again with a new story."

The next morning, Dickens arrived at Arthur's toy factory promptly at nine. We offered him tea and pastries, then took him on a brief tour of the premises. He was thrilled with the craftsmanship, but positively overwhelmed to find himself in the presence of the man he kept referring to as "King Arthur."

"Just yesterday, you didn't seem surprised to meet Father Christmas," I said jokingly. "Now, you're almost hopping up and down in your excitement at meeting my old friend and helper. Why, my feelings might be hurt!"

"It's just that I always thought you existed, but never suspected King Arthur did," Dickens babbled.

Arthur was red-faced with embarrassment. "Please calm yourself, Mr. Dickens," he suggested. "When time permits, I'll be glad to tell you about my real experiences, if you like, not those grand, made-up adventures you've apparently heard and believed. For now, I think we all should listen to Santa—Father Christmas—because he has an idea for you."

"I enjoyed reading your Christmas stories last night, and truly believe you are one of the finest writers ever to live on this Earth," I began, and it was Dickens's turn to blush. "I found 'The Goblins Who Stole a Sexton' to be especially good, but I think most readers would find it less a tale about Christmas than a ghost story that accidentally took place on December twenty-fifth. Why not take the best parts of that story—the mean-tempered man who hated the Christmas joy of others, and his nighttime visitors who changed his ways—and build a whole new book around them, making certain this time that every reader would realize the author is delivering a message about Christmas, and how everyone should celebrate it!"

Dickens smiled and replied, "Why, that's exactly what I'll do! It will be a few months before I begin, of course. Right now, I'm writing a novel called *Martin Chuzzlewit* and I must finish that book first."

Arthur said quickly, "Mr. Dickens, in ten weeks it will be December twenty-fifth. You'll find that, when working with Father Christmas, people can accomplish things in a tenth of the time normal jobs take to be done. If you mean what you say about loving Christmas and wanting to restore it again in England, I suggest you drop everything else and begin writing the story Father Christmas has suggested."

Arthur's voice had a tone of great authority; Dickens was visibly impressed. "I'll do exactly as you say, King Arthur."

I added, "Mr. Dickens, I don't know your normal method of writing. I believe, though, if you close yourself in your study with a good supply of paper, ink, and quill pens, you'll find you have all the inspiration, energy, and time you need."

Dickens hurried away. We waited, not wanting to contact him for fear of disturbing his writing. Then, late one night during the second week of November, there was a knock on Arthur's door. Charles Dickens came in clutching a cloth sack.

"I've brought you the manuscript of my new book," he said nervously. "I have no idea whether it's good or not. Every day as I sat at my desk it seemed as though an invisible hand gripped mine and made my pen write unexpected words at terrifying speed. If you would, please read this book, and when you've finished come call on me at my home and tell me what you think. Its title is *A Christmas Carol*."

So that night Arthur, Layla, and I read all about Ebenezer Scrooge and the ghosts who came to visit him. We spent hours laughing and crying and finally rejoicing when the old man repented his meanness and promised to forever "keep Christmas in his heart."

The next morning we hurried to Dickens's house. Although it was early, his wife and children were already gone. Dickens asked us to come inside, offered us refreshments, then blurted, "Is my story all right?"

"Is it all right?" Arthur asked incredulously. "Mr. Dickens, you have written the finest story of Christmas that will ever be printed on a page! Bless you, sir, and may you feel great satisfaction for a job well done!"

I echoed Arthur's sentiments, but Layla hesitated.

"I agree *A Christmas Carol* is wonderful, Mr. Dickens," she observed, "and I hope I might mention one small concern without seeming unappreciative of your effort."

"Newspaper critics have said many harsh things about my work," Dickens chuckled. "Please, say whatever you like."

"This concerns the crippled son of Scrooge's employee Bob Cratchit," my wife explained. "He's a wonderful boy as you describe him, and I'm so glad he doesn't die as Scrooge once foresaw, but I just don't think you've given him an appropriate name."

"You mean Little Fred?" Dickens asked. "I chose that name because it's so common. Everyone who reads *A Christmas Carol* will know someone named Fred."

"That's just the problem," Layla said. "Your story is wonderfully uncommon, and so are the names of the rest of your characters— 'Ebenezer Scrooge,' 'Jacob Marley.' The very names of the ghosts of Christmas Past, Present, and Future will help readers picture them in their minds. But 'Little Fred' lacks any flair, and I'm afraid his character will be overlooked as a result."

"My wife never offers criticism without a solution, as well," I told Dickens. "Layla, do you perhaps have another name to suggest?"

"The child should have a name that springs from the tongue," she replied. "I've always loved the sound of the letter 'T,' and I wonder if you might consider renaming your character 'Tiny Tim'?"

"It's perfect!" Dickens barked, and snatching his manuscript from Arthur's hand, he took a quill pen and made the necessary corrections immediately.

Everything went rapidly after that. To help keep down the price of the book and make it affordable to even the poorest readers, we provided Charles Dickens with money to pay some of the cost of having *A Christmas Carol* printed. It was published shortly before Christmas in that year of 1843 and was an instant sensation. Christmas 1844 found all of England ready to celebrate the holiday again with open joy and merry festivities. Father Christmas was once again welcome in almost every English home, and it was a special thrill for me to deliver those presents.

We'd hoped Charles Dickens would eventually join us forever, but this was not to be. He had other books to write and, only a year after *A Christmas Carol* was published, tried his luck with another holiday tale, *The Chimes*. Dickens told friends that this new work "knocked the *Carol* out of the field," but of course this didn't happen. Charles Dickens went on to write several great books, *David Copperfield* being perhaps the best, but he had already outdone any writers of the past or future in creating the finest Christmas fiction possible. Certainly for the rest of his life Charles Dickens was identified with Christmas, and this was only right.

Layla and I stayed with Arthur for several more years, enjoying the pleasant task of gift-giving in a country where we'd too long been unwelcome. Just as I was beginning to think of myself as Father Christmas instead of Santa, the urge came upon us to return to America. Felix, Leonardo, Sarah, Willie Skokan, and Ben Franklin undoubtedly had things under control there, but that exciting new nation was certain to suffer the inevitable pains of political and social growth. We wanted to be there, and took a steamship back across the Atlantic.

Dr. O'Hanlon wasn't an evil man, just a skeptical one. Although he no
longer believed in me, he didn't want to make Virginia sad. So he suggested
she write a letter to the "Question and Answer" section editor
of the *New York Sun* newspaper asking him if I existed.

TWENTY-TWO

"Yes, Virginia, There Is a Santa Claus"

elcome back!" Felix called out as Layla and I stepped off the ramp of the steamship and onto the dock in New York harbor in the spring of 1860. "The reindeer missed you. The rest of us did, too, of course."

We had to take a series of trains from New York to Cooperstown. Willie Skokan was waiting there at the station with a horse-drawn carriage. After we'd loaded our luggage and climbed aboard, it was still another hour-long drive to our farmhouse. Ben Franklin, Leonardo, and Sarah greeted us there, along with someone we'd never met. Layla and I were struck by his dark, intelligent eyes and the bright cloth turban wound around his head.

"This is Sequoyah, a Cherokee who invented an alphabet so his people could have a written language as well as a spoken one," Ben explained.

Sequoyah smiled and shook our hands. "I see you're staring at my scarf," he said politely to Layla. "Not all Indians wear feathers and headdresses, you know. This cloth keeps my head protected from the sun when it's hot, and from the dampness when it's raining."

"It's a very attractive scarf," Layla said politely. "I didn't mean to stare; I haven't met many Indians before."

"Except for the color of our skin, we're the same as you," Sequoyah replied. "Sadly, many people don't understand that."

"Sequoyah can't even go to town since many people there insult him because he's an Indian," Sarah said sharply. "It's disgraceful. Felix and I first met him in Washington, D.C., where he was representing his tribe in 1829, when the government decided to force the Cherokee to move from their homes in North Carolina to Oklahoma."

"I didn't do a very good job of representing," Sequoyah admitted. "We were forced to move anyway. Many of us died on the way. The Cherokee now call that journey 'The Trail of Tears.' "

"We've always made a point of giving gifts to the Cherokee children on that Oklahoma reservation ever since," Sarah continued. "After you left for England, we were able to convince Sequoyah to come and join us, so his talents can be useful forever."

"Soon I hope to translate Mr. Dickens's wonderful story *A Christmas Carol* into the Cherokee alphabet," Sequoyah said. "The children in our tribe will love it."

"Isn't it a terrible thing that this intelligent, gifted man can't even walk into a store in our village and be treated like everyone else?" Sarah asked indignantly.

"There's more trouble coming about skin color, and soon," Willie Skokan said solemnly, and we all were surprised because Willie seldom said much, preferring to listen to the rest of us. "The coming war's all about the slaves. It will be terrible."

Willie wouldn't say any more, so Felix offered details. "Santa, Layla, so much has happened since you've been gone. Abraham Lincoln's just been elected president. All of the Southern states are going to try and leave the Union because their citizens believe slavery won't be allowed anymore. President Lincoln won't let the states leave—*secede* is the word being used—so everyone expects there will be a civil war, with the Northern states fighting the Southern ones. Slavery is the worst thing in the history of the world," he concluded, sounding bitter.

I wondered for a moment at the anger and pain in his voice, then remembered Felix had once been a slave himself.

The United States had been steadily expanding to the west, Felix explained. Where the original thirteen colonies had mostly hugged the Atlantic coast and extended partially inland, now American explorers and settlers were swarming all the way to the far Pacific Ocean.

"In 1847, only twenty thousand people lived in the region called California," Felix said. "In 1848, gold was discovered there. By 1852, two hundred fifty-five thousand people had settled in California."

"Our gift-giving will have to cover a lot more territory," I said thoughtfully.

"We'll have plenty of time to plan," Felix predicted glumly. "This so-called civil war has got to come soon, and I expect it to last for a long while. Since war reduces our special powers, many American children will wait in vain for Santa until the fighting is finally over."

Felix was right. The Civil War broke out in April 1861 and lasted until 1865. All wars are terrible, but this one was worse than most. Families argued over the issue of slavery, and sometimes brothers fought on opposing sides. Battles raged across the country. As far as gift-giving was concerned, we had to content ourselves with delivering presents to those areas where armies weren't lurking.

But even while my friends and I were so limited, the story of Santa Claus became more widespread. Soldiers in both armies dressed up like me on Christmas Day to hand out presents to their comrades. Books, magazines, and newspapers contained stories about me, made-up stories where I did amazing things. Often these stories were accompanied by pictures, and no two pictures were alike. Some artists drew me rail-thin, others roly-poly. Sometimes I had a long white beard and other times just a mustache and goatee. The reindeer and sleigh made popular by Clement Moore's poem were always shown, though.

And the renewed holiday spirit in England caused by *A Christmas Carol* continued to flourish. In 1862, a British company even printed and sold something called "Christmas cards," cards wishing people "A Happy Christmas" or "A blessed New Year."

It took another dozen years for the idea to catch on in America, but once it did every family seemed to send Christmas cards to friends and loved ones. It was a fine new tradition.

Arthur, Francis, Attila, and Dorothea pleaded with the rest of us to leave America and return to Europe, but there were always wars there, too. The eight of us in the United States were determined to bide our time until the Civil War was finally over. But when it was, in 1865, bad feelings remained between the North and South. President Lincoln, who might have been able to help both sides work out their problems, was assassinated less than a week after Confederate General Robert E. Lee surrendered to Union General Ulysses S. Grant. The next few years were difficult for everyone.

We did our best to help heal the country, hoping to remind everyone that Christmas is the season of forgiveness and love by bringing our gifts to as many children as possible every Christmas Eve. My team of reindeer whirled me all over the night skies, and the rest of the group fanned out across the country to deliver their loads of toys by less spectacular means. Still, we found we couldn't cover all the necessary territory if we kept our only base in upstate New York. Fortunately, in 1869 the first railroad tracks were completed that linked the American East and West. In 1872, Yellowstone became the first American national park, a lovely area of wild, natural beauty. Its trees, lakes, mountains, and wild animals were protected by the government. Quietly, Sarah, Sequoyah, and Willie Skokan established another base for us there.

Great strides were made in science. Alexander Graham Bell invented the telephone in 1876. Three years later, Thomas Edison perfected the first electric lamp. Seventeen years after that, Henry Ford built his first automobile.

America was becoming a modern country. But as people learned more about science, they somehow began to doubt things that couldn't be explained with formulas and blueprints. They lost the ability to know the difference between illusion and magic.

"This is getting ridiculous," Ben Franklin announced one day in the autumn of 1896. "Adults all over this country are deciding there can't really be a Santa Claus because he wasn't created by a scientist. Why, Leonardo da Vinci, the greatest scientist of all time, is the one who made it possible for reindeer to fly! For two cents I'd grab all the grown-ups in America and make them take a long ride in your sleigh!"

"They wouldn't all fit," Leonardo said helpfully. He didn't understand sarcasm; many scientists don't. "If you really want to have all of them flying with the reindeer at once, I'll have to build a much larger sleigh, and carve bigger wings for the sleigh and the reindeer."

Layla looked up from a book she was reading and said, "At least most newspapers and magazines aren't against us, Ben. Why, many of them publish lovely stories about Santa, and Thomas Nast at the *Harper's Weekly* draws those wonderful Santa cartoons."

"I don't think they're wonderful," I grumbled. "He makes me look too fat, and he draws me the size of an elf instead of a man."

"Blame Clement Moore for that," Layla reminded me. "He called you an elf in his poem."

"That's no excuse," I replied, irritated at the thought. Not only were Nast's cartoons unflattering about my height and weight, they had proven so popular with readers that, all across America, anyone familiar with them assumed this was exactly the way I looked. Worse, except for the height, Layla and the others kept insisting that was the way I *did* look.

"Let's get back to the adults who no longer believe," Felix urged. "Many of these adults are fathers and mothers. When they have doubts about Santa, those doubts are often shared with their children. And that, my friends, is a disgrace! To think that some children no longer believe in Santa Claus! Something has to be done!"

We tried to calm Ben and Felix down, reminding them that many grown-ups, far from disbelieving, were doing their best to contribute to universal holiday good spirits.

"Remember Ralph E. Morris of the New England Telephone Company?" Layla asked. "He's the one who looked at those strings of electric lights on telephone switchboards and suggested they be hung on Christmas trees. Those make such a nice display! And there's that police commissioner in New York City—what was his name?"

"Theodore Roosevelt," Leonardo said, looking up for a moment from a diagram he was drawing in a notebook. I glanced at the diagram, which was of a giant sleigh. Apparently Leonardo was getting ready just in case we did decide to take all the adults in America on a ride through the sky with our reindeer.

"Yes, Commissioner Roosevelt," Layla continued. "During the Christmas season he likes to go out in the city streets and lead carolers in singing that new song, 'One Horse Open Sleigh,' that many prefer to call 'Jingle Bells.' And, of course, there's Thomas Nast."

"Nast's cartoons are ridiculous," Felix snapped.

"Because they make me look short and fat?" I asked hopefully.

"No, because the man draws us living at the North Pole!" Felix replied. "Isn't that the most foolish thing? Nobody's even been able to reach the North Pole. Robert Peary's tried and failed. I think Nast and all the doubting adults ought to be sent there. A little snow and ice might do them good. No one could live at the North Pole!"

"Oh, I think I could," Leonardo said quickly. "In fact, I have a diagram here that shows how—"

"Later, please, Leonardo," Felix interrupted. "Santa, what can we do to make everyone believe in you again?"

"I don't think we can do anything, Felix," I answered softly. "I can't go out and fly my sleigh in front of every doubting grown-up and child in America. Even with our powers, there's just not enough time. If it's meant for these disbelievers to start believing again, someone else will have to make them do it for us."

Just a year later, someone did. Two someones, really.

The first someone was an eight-year-old girl named Virginia O'Hanlon, who lived in New York with her parents. Virginia's father considered himself a man of science. He was a doctor who sometimes advised Commissioner Theodore Roosevelt and the rest of the New York City Police Department. Dr. O'Hanlon decided there wasn't any Santa Claus, although I had personally come to his house on several Christmas Eves to leave presents in Virginia's stocking. Perhaps

Dr. O'Hanlon didn't talk much to Mrs. O'Hanlon, and thought she left the gifts for their daughter. In any event, some of Virginia's friends at school wondered out loud if there really was a Santa Claus, and when she got home that afternoon she asked her father whether or not I was real.

Dr. O'Hanlon wasn't an evil man, just a skeptical one. Although he no longer believed in me, he didn't want to make Virginia sad. So he suggested she write a letter to the "Question and Answer" section editor of the *New York Sun* newspaper asking him if I existed. I don't think he ever expected Virginia to write that letter, but she did.

Virginia's letter read:

> *Dear Editor:*
>
> *I am eight years old, and some of my little friends say there is no Santa Claus. Papa says, "If you see it in the Sun, it's so." Please tell me the truth, is there a Santa Claus?"*
>
> *Virginia O'Hanlon*

Now, the "Question and Answer" editor of the *New York Sun* was a man named Francis Church. Mr. Church had once been a famous reporter, but now he had what the newspaper considered an unimportant job. Sometimes Mr. Church answered questions in ways that made readers of the *Sun* very angry. It's possible he didn't like his job very much at all.

But Francis Church did love Christmas, and he did believe in me. Maybe it was the marbles I'd left for him one Christmas Eve when he was a boy. In any event, on September 21, 1897, Mr. Church printed Virginia's letter and his answer to it right on the editorial page of his newspaper, where untold thousands of people read them.

Mr. Church's reply was so perfect I found myself wondering if Felix and Ben Franklin might have written it for him. It began:

Virginia, your little friends are wrong. They have been affected by the skepticism of a skeptical age. They do not believe, except they see . . .

Yes, Virginia, there is a Santa Claus. He exists as certainly as love and generosity and devotion exist, and you know how they abound and give to your life its highest beauty and joy. Alas! How dreary would the world be if there were no Santa Claus. . . . You might get your papa to hire men to watch all the chimneys on Christmas Eve to catch Santa Claus, but even if you did not see Santa Claus coming down, what would that prove? Nobody sees Santa Claus, but that is no sign that there is no Santa Claus. The most real things in the world are those that neither children nor men can see . . .

No Santa Claus? Thank God, he lives and lives forever. A thousand years from now, Virginia, nay, ten times ten thousand years from now, he will continue to make glad the heart of childhood.

I don't know if Virginia cried when she read Mr. Church's answer to her letter, but I certainly did. I cried with joy, because I knew anyone reading those beautiful words would believe in me again and never stop believing in me anymore. The editors at the *Sun* must have thought so, too, because they reprinted Virginia's letter and Mr. Church's reply every Christmas season for the next fifty-two years, until the paper was finally closed down.

Virginia herself became a teacher, and a very good one, who

always told her students they should believe in me. After teaching in public schools for a while, she taught in a school for children who were very, very sick. Virginia's special pupils there were always visited by me or my helpers on Christmas Eve.

Of course, I'd long had a rule about giving my gifts only to children, not grown-ups, but I decided to make one exception. On Christmas morning 1897, Mr. Church awoke to find the finest set of marbles ever made had been left in a new stocking tacked up by his fireplace. There was also a note that said simply, "Thank you. Love, Santa."

That same Christmas morning found Layla, Ben Franklin, Leonardo, Felix, and me back at the Cooperstown farmhouse, worn out from our gift-giving activities of the night before. As we sipped cocoa before enjoying some well-earned sleep, Ben commented, "I truly believe that letter from Virginia and Mr. Church's answer may have done the trick! More children than ever believe in you, Santa."

"And though that's a problem we're glad to have, it's still a problem," Felix noted. "It soon will be impossible to keep track of all the children who believe in you, and all those children must get presents. It's awkward being so far away from our friends in Yellowstone National Park, from Arthur and Francis in London, and from Attila and Dorothea in Nuremberg. It would be so much more efficient if we could all work together in one place. But I wonder, where could that place be?"

"Thomas Nast has shown us," Leonardo blurted. "Do you have time to listen to me now? In Nast's cartoons, Santa lives at the North Pole, and for the reasons I'm about to share with you, I think the North Pole would be perfect. . . ."

"Santa Claus! Bully!" the president blurted, peering at me from behind tiny, round-lensed eyeglasses. At first I was offended, thinking he was accusing me of picking on someone, but then I remembered that "bully" was his favorite expression of excitement and pleasure.

TWENTY-THREE

Theodore Roosevelt and
Our North Pole Home

n the late 1800s, the North Pole seemed like a very mysterious place. Everyone knew it existed, but no one had ever been there. It was the absolute top of the Earth, a region of snow and wind and bitter cold, scientists said, destined by its unique location to have months where the sun would not shine at all, followed by six months of constant sunlight. When he drew his cartoons of Santa living there, Thomas Nast thought it was a joke. But Leonardo da Vinci didn't.

"Consider the location, Santa Claus," Leonardo pleaded with me during early 1898, just a few months after Virginia O'Hanlon's letter to the *New York Sun* inspired new widespread belief in me. "The number of children we must serve grows every year. We can't continue to have some of our helpers in one place and some in another. Besides, it's becoming harder to keep the locations of our toy factories and reindeer barn secret. With so many people around, there's less privacy. At the North Pole we could all work together again as one team, and few, if any, visitors would disturb us."

"What about all the snow, Leonardo, and what about the ice?" I protested. "I have wonderful friends, gifted individuals like you—but no one among us is a penguin."

"Penguins only inhabit cold areas in the Southern Hemisphere," Leonardo said helpfully.

"Oh, you know very well what I mean," I huffed, but in the end I gave Leonardo permission to study how a permanent Santa headquarters might be established at the North Pole. He quickly traveled to New York City to meet with Robert Peary, a civil engineer who was determined to become the first person ever to reach the North Pole. Such visits to people involved in projects he found interesting were common for Leonardo. About this same time, he frequently made his way to Dayton, Ohio, where, in his words, he "helped out" brothers Orville and Wilbur Wright. Leonardo said he liked visiting the brothers because they were experts at building and repairing bicycles, a new form of two-wheeled, self-pedaled transportation that had become very popular with children. But the rest of us suspected our old friend was curious about how long it might take the Wrights to invent an airplane using the same principles of flight Leonardo had applied to my sleigh and reindeer so many years earlier.

While he traveled and studied, the rest of us went on about our increasingly complicated business. Earning the money to pay for our mission became harder every year. We certainly weren't the only toy manufacturers in the world anymore. It also was necessary to constantly monitor countries where we wanted to give gifts, but were kept from doing so by revolutions and other political problems. Russia, for instance, had a great religious tradition that included extended celebrations of Christ's birth, but more and more it seemed a possible new government there might discourage these celebrations, and, indeed, religious freedom altogether.

And in 1898, America got itself into another war, this time with Spain, though the conflict's few battles between April, when war was declared, and August, when a treaty was signed, were all fought on islands adjacent to the United States—Puerto Rico and Cuba. Theodore Roosevelt, the former New York City police commissioner whom Layla had so much admired, turned out to be the dominant figure in the Spanish-American War, leading a troop of soldiers he called the "Rough Riders" on a charge up San Juan Hill in Puerto Rico that thrilled his fellow Americans. Soon afterward, Roosevelt was elected governor of New York, then vice president of the United States. He became president in 1901 after the assassination of William McKinley. When Roosevelt assumed the office of president, I decided to carry out a plan I'd long been considering.

"I'm off to Washington, D.C.," I told the others in the spring of 1902. "It's been obvious to me for some time that, in order to properly carry out our mission around the world, we'll need to make ourselves known to leaders of governments. That way, we'll be welcome wherever we go and not suspected of being invaders or spies. President Theodore Roosevelt seems to be a person of intelligence and imagination. I want to tell him about us first, and then get his help in introducing us to the other world leaders."

It was a simple matter to take the train to Washington and arrange an appointment with the president. Government wasn't so complicated then. In fact, it was a tradition that once a year the White House was opened to the public, and thousands of men and women lined up to walk through it and shake the president's hand.

When I was ushered into President Roosevelt's office, he got up from behind his desk and, like Charles Dickens sixty years earlier, recognized me right away.

"Santa Claus! Bully!" the president blurted, peering at me from behind tiny, round-lensed eyeglasses. At first I was offended, thinking he was accusing me of picking on someone, but then I remembered that "bully" was his favorite expression of excitement and pleasure.

"Thank you for seeing me, Mr. President," I began. "I've come to ask for your help—"

"Not at all, Santa, not at all!" He grinned. "Do call me Theodore, won't you? Say, let me send for some cocoa and cookies. You do like cocoa and cookies, don't you? I used to leave them out for you every Christmas when I was a boy. Oh, this is bully! You say you want my help? Anything, my friend, anything! Let's get our refreshments and talk all about it!"

I ended up spending several days with Theodore. He insisted that I be his guest at the White House and introduced me to his wife and children, all of whom were as energetic and outgoing as their father. Theodore didn't tell his family who I really was, of course, simply saying I was Mr. Nicholas from upper New York State who'd come to work out some land problems. Mrs. Roosevelt and most of the children seemed to accept this, but I caught one of the Roosevelt daughters, Alice, watching me closely and taking special note of my white beard and somewhat generous waistline. I think she knew.

Theodore himself I found delightful, despite his outspoken love for war and fighting. Though tremendously intelligent, the president had somehow retained the enthusiasm of a young boy. He immediately announced he would give up politics so he and his entire family could join us in our mission. It took me some time to convince him that the country needed him as president more.

"Well, could you at least name a toy after me?" Theodore pleaded, and I was happy to oblige. The most popular toy of 1903 became the teddy bear, which was named after Theodore in honor of his great interest in animals. Theodore even looked a little like a bear, with his bristling brown mustache and somewhat prominent teeth.

Theodore was happy to help me make contact with other world leaders, and in several cases used a combination of personal charm and polite threats to make them agree to assist me and my helpers whenever we required it.

That dilemma solved, I told Theodore a little about our problems in establishing a central headquarters and toy factory. He suggested we simply move into the White House—"Plenty of room here, just plenty, and wouldn't it be bully to have you and Ben Franklin and Leonardo da Vinci and the others under the same roof with me?"

"Thank you for the offer, Theodore, but it wouldn't be right for us to seem to belong more to one country than any other," I explained. "As it is, we will never be able to deliver gifts to every deserving child everywhere, since our powers are limited by wars and because some parents prefer we don't visit their homes. If we lived in the White House with you, children in other countries might think we favored American children above any others, and, as you know, we love all children equally."

"Well, the North Pole certainly isn't the property of any single nation, but it's a very cold place, and unfit for humans," Theodore replied. "I don't care how intelligent your Leonardo da Vinci is, he'll be hard-pressed to invent some way for you and your helpers to live up there, let alone reach it in the first place. Tell you what: We'll get you together with Robert Peary and perhaps you can find some way to reach the North Pole successfully. That would be a good start, wouldn't it?"

It didn't seem polite to tell the president that Leonardo already had been talking to Robert Peary. Theodore wrote me a letter of introduction, which I didn't have to use; Leonardo invited Peary to visit us at the Cooperstown farmhouse. He seemed very discouraged when he arrived.

"I've made several unsuccessful expeditions," Peary complained. "Something always goes wrong. We head north from Canada or Alaska, and then we run out of food, or important equipment breaks down. It's depressing."

"Why go to so much trouble just to get to a place that really isn't that important?" Layla asked. "I realize the North Pole is the top of the world, but, after all, once you did get there all you could do is plant a flag or something."

Peary's eyes gleamed. "It's a matter of being first, Mrs. Claus, of doing something no one else in the whole history of the world has ever done before."

"We know all about that," Felix commented dryly.

In any event, Peary agreed Leonardo could come with him on his next attempt to reach the North Pole. That one didn't succeed, either, but Leonardo came back convinced that the North Pole would make the perfect home base for us.

"Once we were settled there, no one would bother us except occasional passing polar bears," he insisted. "There would be so much space. We could make our toy factories as large as we wanted."

"It would be impossible for our craftsmen to build toys if they were exposed to freezing winds and blizzards," commented Arthur, who was visiting us from England. "The strongest-walled houses would blow down in some of those Arctic storms. Besides, none of us knows how to make an igloo."

"We'd use the principle of igloos, not igloos themselves," Leonardo urged. "We'll create a man-made, self-contained environment.

See, the snow and ice can be used as insulation. You must factor in density; let me write out the formula." He did, and it was the strangest set of unreadable chicken scratchings I'd ever seen.

"You've lost me," I admitted.

Ben Franklin took the notebook from Leonardo, glanced at the scribbled formula, and said, "Basically, Santa, Leonardo wants to use the snow and ice as outer walls to protect us from the bad weather. As an outer shell, so to speak. Inside that shell, we can build roofs and walls, toy factories and apartments."

"We can use generators to supply power," Leonardo added. "There aren't any portable generators yet, but I'll invent them immediately. I have some ideas, too, for other inventions that will eventually allow us to get energy from the sun itself, or, rather, from the light it radiates. Just let us locate the right spot at the North Pole, Santa, and I'll teach the craftsmen from our toy factories to build the finest snow- and ice-covered facility possible.

"By the way, there's one more advantage," he continued. "If our outer shell is made up of snow, ice, and earth, then, in the near future when airplanes fly all over the skies, pilots looking down at the North Pole won't be able to tell anyone is living there at all. They'll just think we're an especially big hill or bit of glacier."

"What do you mean, airplanes flying all over the skies?" I asked peevishly, since I didn't really understand anything else Ben or Leonardo had said.

"Oh, it will happen, Santa," Leonardo assured me. "In fact, just before Christmas this year I'm going to go to Kitty Hawk, North Carolina, with my friends the Wright brothers. They think they might be able to make their airplane fly there. I could, of course, tell them exactly what to do, but I think it's better for them to figure things out for themselves with just a few hints from me."

I snorted, less from disbelief than from a growing sense that someday soon I'd be living at the North Pole. Leonardo had proven through the centuries that he was capable of solving any scientific problem.

The Wright brothers became famous at Kitty Hawk on December 17, 1903, when their primitive engine-powered airplane first flew 120 feet in twelve seconds, then 852 feet in fifty-nine seconds. It was hard for me to feel too impressed; every Christmas season, I flew thousands of miles in my sleigh. Later on, in history books for schoolchildren, there were photographs of that airplane and the Wright brothers standing beside it. If you study some of those photographs carefully, you'll see a tall, slender man in the background. It's Leonardo, of course.

Leonardo came back to the Cooperstown farm from Kitty Hawk and set to work inventing plans for our new North Pole home. It took him more than five years. In the meantime, Theodore was elected president for a full four-year term, and he kept pestering me to give up the idea of the North Pole and move into the White House instead.

"What I'll do is make the Congress vote that you and your helpers can live there no matter who is president," he promised.

"But, Theodore, you can't tell Congress all about us," I reminded him. "Some of those elected officials wouldn't be able to keep our secrets."

Theodore frowned. "I would threaten to shoot anyone who told on you. They know I'd do it, too."

"Please don't," I asked. "Besides, Leonardo's determined that we're going to go and live with the polar bears."

"Well, let me finish this term as president and I'll move up there with you," Theodore suggested. "Things around here are getting too civilized. You might need someone to protect you from the polar bears. I'd like to shoot a polar bear or two."

"We can talk more about that when the time comes," I suggested. "Right now, the country and the world need you more." Theodore seemed pleased when I said that; he always enjoyed praise.

Finally, in early 1909, after several months of building odd-looking igloos in the fields of our farm, Leonardo announced he had perfected what he called his "self-contained environment" plans and was ready to proceed. We knew from the newspapers that Robert Peary planned to make his next attempt to reach the North Pole in March. We contacted him, and he invited Leonardo to go along, as well as anyone else from our group who wanted to come. Willie Skokan did, of course, and so did Arthur and Attila, who always craved new adventures. Disgustingly, Layla wanted to go, too, which meant I was expected to go with her.

"I hope you're satisfied," I grumbled four weeks later, as all of us in Peary's group huddled in drafty igloos. We were swaddled in fur cloaks provided by Eskimos; I later found they treated the fur with fish oil, which made the cloaks waterproof and very, very smelly. After spending three weeks in the cold and snow, Peary still thought we were another two weeks away from the North Pole.

"Oh, stop complaining," Layla said sharply. "Leonardo thinks he found an error in Peary's map. We'll be at the North Pole in just a few days, he says. So eat a little smoked caribou meat and get some sleep."

"I'd rather have cocoa and cookies," I mumbled.

Six days later, on April 6, 1909, Peary and Leonardo, who were walking a few hundred yards ahead of the rest of us, suddenly stopped in their tracks. Peary jumped up and down for joy. "It's the

North Pole! We're here!" he shouted. Personally, I didn't see any real cause for excitement. Where we were looked no different than anywhere else as far as the eye could see—just more snow and ice. But apparently it was the North Pole, and we were there. Peary planted an American flag, which the wind promptly knocked down and blew away. Then we turned around and headed back.

When we returned to civilization, Peary went to New York City and reported his achievement. A few months later another explorer named Frederick Cook, a doctor who had previously traveled with Peary, claimed he had reached the North Pole first. If he had, we hadn't seen him, and he hadn't left behind any markers to prove he'd been there. A fierce debate followed, with some people believing Peary and some believing Cook. We stayed out of it.

For the next four years, Leonardo, Willie Skokan, Arthur, Attila, and dozens of our best craftsmen would head for the North Pole right after we'd completed our holiday season gift-giving. Eventually, Leonardo and some of the craftsmen stayed there year-round. Whenever I asked if I could come and see what they were doing, I was informed they were working hard, didn't need to be interrupted, and would invite me when they were ready. I waited impatiently. So did Theodore, who desperately wanted to be part of what he called "the bully Santa Claus adventure." He left the presidency in 1909 and traveled around the world. Bored, he returned to run for president in 1913, but lost. Theodore then resumed his requests to join us.

"Wait a while longer," I urged. "When the time is right, I'll tell you."

Finally, in May 1913, Leonardo returned to the Cooperstown farm. He told everyone else to pack their belongings and come with him, then instructed me to wait three weeks and fly to the North Pole with the reindeer.

"How will I find you?" I asked. "From the air, I won't be able to tell one snowdrift from another."

"Trust the reindeer and the stars," Leonardo said mysteriously. "When you've acted on faith before, you've always succeeded, haven't you?"

So I spent three weeks all alone, the first time I'd been by myself for so long in centuries. It was quite peaceful; I fed the reindeer and ignored cablegrams from Theodore begging me to let him stow away on the sleigh.

On the appointed day I got up well before dawn, so the reindeer and I could fly away under cover of darkness. Not a stick of furniture or scrap of food was left in the farmhouse. I put my red Santa outfit on over my regular clothes. Somehow when I was up in the sleigh, the red suit seemed to protect me from the weather.

The reindeer and I flew north, and gradually the land beneath us changed from green grass to brown hills and, finally, to rocky ground with patches of snow and ice. I had learned from Leonardo that even the North Pole wasn't always cold and freezing. Sometimes the temperature reached forty degrees, and bits of stringy grass popped up and waved in the wind.

And that was how it looked below as the reindeer and I moved into what was called the Arctic Circle, flying farther north as the sky around us darkened and stars began to twinkle. I watched the stars, and it gradually occurred to me that several of them seemed to shine all in a row, a neat row pointing down. Then I looked at where those stars seemed to be pointing, and there was the tiny figure of Leonardo da Vinci waving at me.

I tugged the reins gently; the reindeer turned downward in a graceful arc. As we drew close, I saw Leonardo was pointing to his left. Doors suddenly swung out of what seemed to be a lumpy hill covered with a layer of snow. Without further direction from me, the reindeer gracefully swooped through the doors and landed on a long, carpeted runway.

I looked around. I was in some sort of enclosed area that seemed to go on forever. It was well lit and warm; as the sleigh came to a stop, Layla and all my old, dear friends—Felix, Attila, Dorothea, Arthur, Francis, Willie Skokan, Ben Franklin, Sarah, Sequoyah, and, of course, Leonardo—crowded around with cries of welcome.

"Come see, Santa, come see!" they chanted like excited children. For the next two hours I was escorted through a wonderland of toy assembly areas, storerooms for tools and raw materials, laboratories, kitchens, dining rooms, bathrooms, guest rooms for visitors, and, finally, private quarters for each of my special friends. It was astonishing, all built under a protective cover of snow and ice and earth, and everything snug and comfortable and somehow welcoming.

"Come over here, Santa, and see your new office," Felix urged, and I found myself in a lovely room with a large desk, couches and overstuffed chairs, bookshelves groaning with volumes of every shape and on every subject, a fireplace with a crackling fire, maps of the world on the walls, an attractive oil painting of Layla—"I do like to keep up my portrait painting," Leonardo confided. "I think this one of Layla is much better than the *Mona Lisa*"—and a wide window offering a panoramic view of the horizon and sky.

"Don't worry about anyone in airplanes being able to look down and see you," Leonardo assured me. "I've invented a type of tinted glass which lets people inside look out, but doesn't let anyone outside look in."

Layla nudged me with her elbow. Actually, she poked me rather sharply. "Thank Leonardo," she commanded in a whisper.

I tried to find the right words and couldn't. Tears came to my eyes, and I reached out and hugged Leonardo da Vinci, the greatest genius who ever lived.

"Is this place all right, Santa?" Leonardo asked anxiously.

"It's better than all right, Leonardo," I answered. "It's home. After all these centuries, after all our wandering, we finally have a home of our own."

Before I could say more, Bill vaulted over the fence. The bull charged.
Almost faster than eyes could see, Bill grabbed the bull's head, bit its lip,
and twisted with his arms, and the bull flopped over on the ground.

TWENTY-FOUR

Happy Christmas to All

e moved just in time. When Theodore ran unsuccessfully in 1913 for a third term as president, he lost to Woodrow Wilson, who promised voters he would keep America out of the awful world war everyone knew was coming.

It came in 1914. The country of Austria-Hungary declared war on Serbia; one after another, more countries became involved, including the United States in 1917. That same year, there was a revolution in Russia. Leaders of the new government soon made it clear they wanted no part of us or our gift-giving.

This sad situation was made a little easier for us by the fact that we were finally away from fighting. No country was especially interested in conquering the North Pole. If, during this war, there were few countries where we could go and give gifts as we pleased, at least we could make toys and wait for peace, which was finally declared in November 1918 after terrible destruction. The war became officially known as World War I, and unofficially nicknamed "the war to end all wars." You know, of course, that it wasn't. Wars still go on today, often in the same countries where World War I was fought. I think we've talked about war long enough. There's not much time left to tell the rest of my story, and there were wonderful things happening, too.

A special moment came in 1919, when we finally allowed Theodore to pack his things and join us. I made the decision a few days after World War I ended. I was visiting Theodore and he talked for a long time about how he'd learned to hate war, too.

"You've never really given me credit for what I did in 1906," Theodore complained. "As president, I helped Russia and Japan work out an agreement that settled their war. I was awarded the Nobel Peace Prize for that effort, I might add."

"Quite true," I agreed. The Nobel Peace Prize was named for Alfred Nobel, a Swedish engineer who'd invented, among other things, dynamite and better gunpowder. He'd come to regret those inventions because of the new violence they made possible, and as a result gave all his money when he died to establish prizes for those who, each year, did the most to bring world peace. Nobel also provided yearly prizes for exceptional achievement in economics, medicine, literature, chemistry, and physics, but the annual Nobel Peace Prize was considered the greatest honor anyone could win.

"Let me come help you, Santa," Theodore continued. "My own son died in this latest war. Let me dedicate myself now to making other people's sons and daughters happy."

I couldn't refuse; when I told Theodore to pack, he whooped like a cowboy. And before daylight on January 6, 1919, I added a final stop on my yearly visit to children in countries where gifts were expected on that date. My sleigh landed right beside Theodore's home. He leaped aboard and positively shouted with glee as I prepared to order the reindeer to fly us away to the North Pole.

"May I, Santa, oh, may I?" Theodore pleaded, and, since I knew what he meant, I nodded.

"Now, Dasher, now, Dancer," hollered President Theodore Roosevelt, naming all eight just the way Clement Moore had first described in his poem. "This is so bully!" Theodore added as we swooped into the night sky.

Sky-swooping soon became more complicated. The first flight credited to the Wright brothers was followed by many more. In 1927, Charles Lindbergh stunned the world by flying his airplane nonstop between New York and Paris. The trip took Lindbergh a little more than thirty-three hours. Up at the North Pole, we were all happy for him, though for us, thanks to Leonardo and his sleigh, flying from New York to Paris took thirty-two hours less.

Lindbergh made the first official long-distance flight, but far from the last. About one year later, a woman named Amelia Earhart joined two men in flying across the Atlantic Ocean in twenty-two hours. I noticed they named their airplane "Friendship." And, as airplanes quickly improved in both power and air speed, people flew farther and faster. In 1932, Amelia Earhart became the first woman to fly alone across the Atlantic, and it took her only thirteen hours and thirty minutes—still not close to our North Pole speed, but respectable enough.

"It seems quite probable that every child in the world will want toy airplanes for Christmas," I predicted over supper in April 1932, about a month before Amelia Earhart made her solo flight. It had been a fine supper; Theodore, who always loved everything to do with the Wild West, had taken a trip to Oklahoma and Texas earlier that year and, in a small Texas town, discovered a cook named Worth, who, Theodore insisted, made the best friend chicken in the world. The rest of us were all especially fond of fried chicken; we visited Worth, sampled his cooking, and immediately talked him into moving to the North Pole with us. Our meals improved considerably, but, after nightly second and third helpings, my waistline didn't.

"Those airplanes are all well and good, but to my mind most boys and girls are soon going to want cowboy toys, too," Theodore argued. "You know, little guns, toy horses, cowboy hats and boots, those sorts of things."

"Perhaps you're right," I admitted. Already, new entertainments called "movies" were very popular, and many of the most popular movies were westerns. Books about cowboys could be found in many homes, too. "Well, Theodore, I suppose you and Sequoyah can advise Willie Skokan and Leonardo and the rest of our craftsmen about how cowboy toys should work and look."

Sequoyah grinned and replied, "I know about alphabets and books, not about cowboys."

To my surprise, Theodore shook his head, too. "Santa, I love cowboys too much to claim to be an expert. We need someone else, a real cowboy, here to help us out, and I have just the cowboy to suggest."

A warm fire was crackling nearby, and we all gathered around Theodore as he told us about the adventures of a man named Bill Pickett, the son of a former slave. Bill Pickett grew up to star in something called "**The 101 Ranch Wild West Show**" and, Theodore claimed, won wrestling matches with wild steers by biting the animals on the lip or nose.

"Oh, be serious, Theodore!" Felix complained. "No self-respecting wild steer could be beaten that way! I always enjoy your tall tales, but this one is just too much. Try telling us another."

"I promise you, it's the truth!" Theodore growled; he hated anyone making fun of him. "What Bill Pickett does is called 'bulldogging,' and besides wild steers, some say he's even wrestled down a buffalo and a bull elk! I understand he's retired from the rodeo now and living on a ranch in Oklahoma. Do let's go find him, Santa. You'll see, Bill Pickett would be a great addition here. I was right about Worth and his fried chicken, wasn't I?"

It was hard to argue with Theodore on that point, especially since I'd just been wondering if I might be able to enjoy one more piece of fried chicken before dessert; the next day Theodore and I left for Chandler, Oklahoma, where Bill Pickett had his ranch. As always on non-holiday trips, we took more common transportation—dogsleds south until civilization, where we switched to trains.

Bill Pickett turned out to be a wonderful man, quite small and wiry, built much like Willie Skokan. And, as Theodore Roosevelt had done a few decades earlier, Bill recognized me right away.

"Why, it's Santa Claus," he chuckled, shaking my hand. "Good to see you down here in Oklahoma!" Actually, it was somewhat surprising no one else had given me a second glance on my trip south to meet Bill. A year earlier, an artist had finally painted me the way I really looked. The Coca-Cola Company had hired a Swedish-American artist, Hans Sundblom, to do a "Santa" painting for a series of holiday advertisements on behalf of their popular American soft drink. Without telling anyone else at the North Pole, I discreetly visited Hans, introduced myself, explained my frustration at constantly being drawn elf-size, and ended up posing for his portraits myself. Hans drew "Santa" ads for Coca-Cola for thirty-five years, and I was his model in every one. We kept my real identity a secret. Whenever Hans had to have other people in his studio at the same time I was there, he introduced me to them as "Les Prentice," a retired salesman. At any rate, I was finally pleased with the way I looked in print.

Bill Pickett's rugged ranch in Oklahoma was a long way from Hans Sundblom's comfortable studio. After telling me, "You sure look like those Coca-Cola pictures," a comment I supposed was meant as a compliment, Bill cheerfully took us out to his corral, where he pointed to a huge, snorting bull.

"Think that one would be hard to wrestle down?" he asked.

"Please don't try, Bill," I said anxiously. "That animal must weigh a thousand pounds. Don't hurt yourself trying to impress us."

Before I could say more, Bill vaulted over the fence. The bull charged. Almost faster than eyes could see, Bill grabbed the bull's head, bit its lip, and twisted with his arms, and the bull flopped over on the ground. Then both the bull and Bill got up, neither worse for the experience, although the bull obviously had learned who was boss.

"So, how was that?" Bill asked, laughing at the expression on my face.

"Bill, we have something important to talk with you about," I replied, and just eleven days later, on April 13, Bill left Chandler to move to the North Pole.

Bill and Ben Franklin almost instantly became best friends. Both were curious about absolutely everything. Whenever Bill took breaks from working in the toy factory with Leonardo, Willie Skokan, and Ben, he got in the habit of visiting me in my study to ask questions.

"You've told me how you can't give holiday presents every year to every child in the world, sometimes because of war or sometimes because parents simply prefer that you don't," he began one day.

I was busy reading letters from children. Thanks to our continued communications with friendly governments around the world, we received regular deliveries of mail at the North Pole, first by dogsled and later by airplane. Bill's question interrupted my reading, but it was a pleasant interruption. "True," I replied.

"Well," Bill continued, "you don't give gifts to grown-ups or even teenagers, usually, so how do you decide when each child should stop getting presents from Santa?"

"I don't decide that," I answered. "It's really decided by the children themselves. You see, there comes a time in the life of each child who truly loves Christmas when that boy or girl realizes even Santa Claus can't give presents to every young person who hopes for one from me. That's when these children gladly give up what I would have brought them in order for boys and girls somewhere else to receive those gifts. It's called generosity of spirit, Bill."

Bill looked a little unhappy. "It surely seems sad, Santa Claus, for those generous young people to end up not getting any gifts themselves, after being so understanding and all."

"That's the wonderful thing about Christmas, Bill!" I exclaimed. "Besides you good friends who live with me here at the North Pole, parents and other adults all over the world are truly Santa's helpers, too! They're proud of their children for making the right, unselfish decision, and they make sure these youngsters continue to get gifts, too. True, the children know their Christmas gifts aren't presents from Santa anymore, but those gifts are just as special as mine because they're given with love, as all gifts should be."

"One question more, Santa," Bill continued. "What if someday, every child in the world made that decision, so that Christmas came and no boys or girls expected you to bring them presents?"

"I don't think that will happen, Bill, and frankly I hope it doesn't,"

I replied. "First, every child who loves the holiday season ought to get some presents from Santa. It's a wonderful, natural thing. Second, not all children make their generous decision at the same age. That's fine, too. It's good we're all a little different. And, finally, you know how I always say my motto is 'It's better to give than to receive.' Well, it's more fun, too. When they believe in me and my presents, it makes me happy. So I don't plan to ever stop giving children gifts!"

"Unless we get this flying problem fixed, you might have to," Felix interrupted. Apparently, he'd been standing in the doorway listening to Bill and me. "Santa, most countries, including some very friendly ones, have rules now about who they allow to fly overhead. 'Restricted air space,' they call it, as though people on the ground also should be able to rule the sky over their heads! Well, they're afraid of bombs, I suppose, and some of them probably wouldn't believe you had a sleigh full of toys instead."

I nodded; it was a very serious problem. "Felix, do you have any suggestions?"

"Well, Layla and I have been talking," he admitted. "You know how she's always admired that woman aviator, the one named Amelia Earhart?"

"And rightly so," I agreed. "Amelia Earhart is clearly the greatest pilot in the world."

"The best pilot in an airplane, but not the best in a sleigh," Bill interrupted quickly, trying to make sure my feelings weren't hurt.

"Probably the best pilot, period," I said firmly. "Don't worry, Bill, I'm not ashamed to admit someone else may be better at something than me. But, Felix, what does Amelia Earhart have to do with our problem?"

"Layla found out Amelia Earhart plans to try to fly all the way around the world," Felix said. "Apparently, Amelia's spent years studying maps of every country. She must know better than anyone else every flight pattern and plane route from one place on Earth to another."

"I'm sure Layla has a reason for thinking this is so important," I commented. "Why hasn't she told me about it herself?"

"Oh, I will, right now," my wife announced, joining Felix, Bill, and me in my study. "And please, Santa, stop asking Worth to fix you extra bedtime snacks. Soon there won't be room in the sleigh for the toys and you at the same time!"

"About Amelia Earhart," I suggested, taking a deep breath and trying, without much success, to suck in my stomach.

"It's very simple," Layla said in the patient tones of a wife who thinks her husband hasn't understood something obvious. "Let's see if Amelia Earhart will become one of our North Pole helpers. Then she can plan all your sleigh routes, working with governments that are friendly and finding ways for you to fly undetected by the unfriendly ones. Don't you remember how Sarah helped us so much when she wrote that first book about traveling around America?"

Stated that way, the solution to our flight problems was very simple. With a little help from the current president—as it happened, he was a distant cousin of Theodore's, named Franklin Roosevelt—we met with Amelia Earhart. She said she'd be honored to join us, and offered to cancel her upcoming round-the-world flight in order to do so.

"That's quite generous, but do you think you might make at least part of that flight?" I asked. "Up at the North Pole we don't have as much information as we should about the islands of the Pacific Ocean. Perhaps if you could explore them before you come to join us, you could help us get gifts delivered to more children in that part of the world."

Amelia said she'd be delighted, if, in turn, we'd allow her to bring her trusty navigator, Frederick Noonan, on the flight with her and later to the North Pole as well. Everything worked out as planned. On July 2, 1937, everyone else in the world except President Roosevelt and those of us at the North Pole thought Amelia Earhart and Frederick Noonan somehow became lost forever on their flight. Actually, they turned north from the Pacific Ocean and flew to join us. We threw a grand party to welcome them, featuring Worth's fried chicken and plenty of homemade chocolate chip cookies for dessert. Layla wanted me to have just one helping of each, but I thought it was only right to have seconds—well, thirds, too—in the proper spirit of celebration.

Bill Pickett

With the help of Amelia and Frederick, I was able to fly my sleigh more efficiently, meaning more children got gifts. This is always our annual goal at the North Pole, to deliver presents to more children than the year before.

Modern technology and better management plans have helped us do this. It finally became necessary to put all our records on computer. Arthur and Francis spent a few decades dividing the countries of the Earth into what they called "regions." Senior staff were each put in charge of a specific region, with the responsibility of recruiting helpers from each country as needed and keeping track of which children wanted what. Arthur naturally oversaw our operations in England, Ireland,

Scotland, and Wales. Francis took Spain and Portugal. Attila and Dorothea directed Germany and Austria, and so on.

We ended up having to divide types of gifts into separate divisions, too, with new helpers to keep track of all the latest developments in their areas of specialization. Zonk and Andy handled drums; Mary Elizabeth and Alison were our doll specialists; Scoop recommended the right books—his favorite was *Beautiful Joe,* the story of a wonderful dog. Bill and Theodore turned down jobs as regional directors to continue being in charge of all cowboy toys. Sequoyah, too, preferred the toy factory to other areas of management; he made it his special concern that our toys reflected the interests of children of all races.

There were other helpers with other jobs; gift-giving started to become complicated with the invention of chimneys so many centuries ago, and never got any simpler. We ended up needing a North Pole library, since we subscribed to many magazines; Marsha was our librarian, and Marilyn our chief researcher. Ira was the North Pole doctor, because even Santa's helpers don't feel well sometimes. Amelia Earhart and Frederick Noonan handled our air travel, and Sarah Kemble Knight decided on all land routes. We even had a public relations department to meet privately with people who didn't understand why Santa Claus should be part of Christmas. This was delicate work sometimes. Leonardo and Willie Skokan ended up having to expand our North Pole home to three times its original size to make room for all the new helpers, but they didn't mind. They were always happiest when there were new chores to be done.

So we became computerized and compartmentalized, but never subsidized. We continued to pay for all our own expenses by inventing ideas for toys and selling some of these ideas to companies in the outside world. For instance, we were delighted when video games became popular. Leonardo and Ben invented literally hundreds of games they sold to outside video-game companies at great profits to us. They thought their best game ever was about a plumber, his brother, and a princess; I always liked the one they invented that involved a hedgehog.

We did most of our toy business with companies in the United States, but had a longtime understanding with the American government that we wouldn't have to pay taxes. Instead, the Internal Revenue Service declared us a "nonprofit" company. From Theodore Roosevelt to the present, every American president has agreed and not bothered us about taxes.

Lately there has been especially good news. Felix and Sarah Kemble Knight came into my study last week and asked if they could speak to me. Both of them were grinning, and Felix announced, "We're going to be married."

"Really?" I asked, delighted at the thought. "When did you decide to get engaged?"

"We've been talking about getting married since the 1800s, but we didn't want to rush into anything," Sarah answered. "Couples really need to take the time to get to know one another before they go racing to the altar. No offense to you and Layla, of course. Sometimes short engagements work out, too."

Later that night I told Layla the happy news, only to be informed she'd known about Felix and Sarah for more than a century.

"Anyone with common sense could tell just by looking at them," Layla said smugly.

"I couldn't tell," I replied, slightly offended.

Layla gave me a warm hug and a kiss. "That's what I love about you, Santa. No one with common sense would have walked out into the night nearly two thousand years ago not knowing what would happen to him, but trusting some higher power would show him how to spend the rest of his life giving gifts and making other people happy. You've got a loving heart, and that's more important than common sense any day."

"I think I have a lot of common sense," I grumbled, but Layla gave me another quick kiss and hurried off to find Sarah and begin planning the wedding.

The marriage took place yesterday. I performed the ceremony. After all, I never really stopped being a bishop. The bride looked beautiful; the groom looked nervous. Afterward, Worth served a huge wedding dinner. Layla thought I ate too much. Everyone at the North Pole went outside into the sparkling snow to wave good-bye to Felix and Sarah as they flew off; I'd lent them my sleigh for their honeymoon. Just before they departed, Amelia consulted her state-of-the-art radar and assured them the weather was perfect all the way from the North Pole to Rome. The pope had invited the newlyweds to stay at one of his mansions there, and Felix wanted to show Sarah where he'd once lived as a slave.

"At least there are no more slaves," I commented to Arthur as we waved good-bye to the rapidly disappearing sleigh. "And maybe one day there'll be no more wars, either."

Then we all went back inside and ate some more. Fried chicken, cocoa, and homemade chocolate chip cookies make the best meal in the world.

Well, that's about all of my story, at least so far. I'm certain there will be more adventures, just as I'm certain there will always be people who truly love Christmas and who, understanding that the main purpose of the holiday is to celebrate the birth of a child and the love he brought with him, have a special place in their hearts for Santa Claus, too.

It's been my pleasure—even more, it's been my honor—to share the holiday spirit with so many of you. Don't ever apologize for loving me as much as I love you. After all, for those who don't want to believe in me, no amount of proof would ever be enough. But for friends like you, who believe what they know to be true in their hearts, no further proof is necessary.

Well, it's getting late. I have many things to do before morning, and you need to be off to bed.

My old friend Clement Moore was the first to write these words as a message from me, and they can't be improved upon, so I'll conclude with them here:

"Happy Christmas to all, and to all a good night."

Santa's Favorite Recipe

WORTH'S NORTH POLE DELIGHT
TENDER FRIED CHICKEN

INGREDIENTS AND SUPPLIES

4 medium or large-size mixing bowls
ice and water
lemon or lime juice
honey (optional)
fresh chicken parts (two to six pieces per diner—
   Santa likes six for his dinner)
salt and fresh ground pepper to taste
   (Santa likes a light seasoning touch)

4 fresh eggs or egg whites
half-cup milk or skim milk
lots of bleached or whole wheat flour
canola, olive, and corn oils
2 large but fairly shallow frying pans,
    preferably with nonstick surface
large platter with plenty of paper towels

PRE-FRYING PREPARATION

1. Buy the freshest whole or cut-up chicken available. Cut into your favorite chicken parts. (Preferred but optional to taste: remove skin and extra fat.) Wash thoroughly in running cold water.
2. Fill one bowl with ice water. Fill second bowl with ice water and lemon or lime juice.
3. In third bowl, gently beat four whole eggs or egg whites with half-cup of milk or skim milk.
4. In fourth bowl, fill with layer of flour.
5. Mix four parts canola oil with one part olive oil and a splash of corn oil in each of the large frying pans. Be sure the pans are only about half-full of oil. Preheat oil mixture in one frying pan. Keep other pan of oil ready for backup.

    Note: You want your chicken pieces to be half under and half out of the oil mixture while frying.

    Caution: Test oil for proper temperature with pinch of flour. If the oil sizzles instantly, it's ready for the chicken.
6. Double-dip chicken in flour: Move chicken from cold-water bath into ice water.

7. From there, remove and dip thoroughly into the egg and milk mixture.

8. Remove and dip it in the flour.

9. Sprinkle lightly with salt and fresh-ground pepper or other spices, as desired. Return seasoned, floured chicken to lemon or lime ice water.

10. Remove quickly and re-dip it in the flour.

    Note: Be ready to pour more flour over chicken for the second dip to get even coating. But even single-dip chicken will be crunchy and tasty.

FRYING

1. Slip floured chicken immediately into the hot oil.

2. If oil gets too hot, it will pop or splatter out of the pan. If so, slightly turn down heat.

3. Keep constant watch on frying chicken. As it begins to brown on one side, turn it over. As it browns on other side, turn again. Turn at least two more times for even frying on both sides.

4. Chicken is ready when it's rich, golden brown, and crisp on both sides, and the sizzle begins to wane. Remove chicken and place on paper-towel-covered platter. Turn over once to let oil drain off both sides. Dab with towels as necessary.

5. If frying a lot of chicken, put second pan of oil on another burner and preheat the oil. As the first oil's frying capacity breaks down, switch frying to the pan of fresh, hot oil. Then empty, clean, and refill the first pan, and preheat another batch of oil for more frying.

    Note: Don't let oil get old and weak while frying.

Caution: Don't cover chicken while it's frying. Don't put finished chicken in warm oven or under heat lamp. Don't cover finished chicken.

6. Serve immediately, fresh fried and hot from the platter.

Note: This is also good as a cold snack later from the fridge. Ask Santa.

Resources

Ball, Ann. *A Litany of Saints*. Huntington, Ind.: Our Sunday Visitor, Inc., 1993.

Barraclough, Geoffrey, ed. *The Times Atlas of World History*. Maplewood, N.J.: Hammond, Inc., 1989.

Crichton, Robin. *Who Is Santa Claus? The True Story Behind a Living Legend*. Edinburgh, Scotland: Canongate Publishing Ltd., 1987.

Cross, F. L. *The Oxford Dictionary of the Christian Church*. New York: Oxford University Press, 1957.

Del Re, Gerard, and Patricia Del Re. *The Christmas Almanack*. New York: Doubleday and Company, 1979.

Ebon, Martin. *Saint Nicholas: Life and Legend*. New York: Harper and Row, 1975.

Encyclopedia Americana. Danbury, Conn.: Americana Corp., 1980.

Garraty, John A., ed. *Encyclopedia of American Biography.* New York: Harper and Row, 1974.

Goldsmith, Terence. *Saints.* New York: Blandford Press Ltd., 1978.

Humble, Richard. *The Travels of Marco Polo.* New York: Franklin Watts, 1990.

Ickis, Marguerite. *The Book of Religious Holidays and Celebrations.* New York: Dodd, Mead, and Company, 1966.

Imbert, Bertrand. *North Pole, South Pole: Journeys to the Ends of the Earth.* New York: Harry N. Abrams, Inc., 1992.

Jackson, Kenneth T., ed. *Atlas of American History.* New York: Charles Scribner's Sons, 1978.

Jones, Charles Williams. *Saint Nicholas of Myra, Bari, and Manhattan.* Chicago, Ill.: University of Chicago Press, 1978.

Jones, E. Willis. *The Santa Claus Book.* New York: Walker and Company, 1976.

Metford, J. C. J. *Dictionary of Christian Lore and Legend.* New York: Thames and Hudson, Inc., 1983.

The National Christmas Tree Association, Milwaukee, Wisconsin.

Professional Rodeo Cowboys Association, Colorado Springs, Colorado.

Sanders, Dennis. *The First of Everything.* New York: Delacorte Press, 1981.

Snyder, Phillip V. *December 25th.* New York: Dodd, Mead, and Company, 1985.

Taylor, Michael J. H., and David Mondey. *Milestones of Flight.* Alexandria, Va.: Jane's Information Group, Inc., 1983.

Weis, Frank W. *Lifelines.* New York: Facts on File, Inc., 1982.

Whyte, Malcolm. *The Meanings of Christmas.* San Francisco, Calif.: Troubador Press, 1973.

The World Book Encyclopedia. Chicago, Ill.: World Book, Inc., 1993.

Acknowledgments

Two people above all others deserve special recognition for helping Santa and me write this book. Besides Layla, it was Mark Hulme who originally urged that it be written. Back in 1994, Susan Besze Wallace was absolutely invaluable, doing an amazing amount of research and making sure all our dates and facts were accurate.

Other special Santa's helpers include Sara Carder, my editor, and Ken Siman, my publicist, at Tarcher/Penguin; Robert Fernandez; Felix Higgins; Del Hillen; Mary Arendes; Art Cory; Don Jesse; Dot and Frank Lauden; Zonk Lanzillo; Rich Billings; Wilson McMillion; Scott Nishimura; Doug Perry; Julie Heaberlin; Rick Press; Charles Caple; Marsha Melton; Mary and Charles Rogers; Ira Hollander; Kelly Goss; Dorit Rabinovitch; Michael and Barbara Rosenberg; Jerry Flemmons; Mike Cochran; Ralph Lauer; Cecil Johnson; Karen Potter; Anita Quinones; John Ryan; Bob and Betty Burns; Jim and Barbara Firth; Buck, Debbie, Jeanne, and Jonathan

Firth; Speaker Jim Wright; Sandy Smith; the Reverend Linda McDermott; Max and Cissy Lale; and Larry Wilson.

Santa dedicates this new edition of his book to everyone who keeps Christmas in his or her heart. I agree, and also dedicate it to Louis and Marie Renz.

Everything I write is always for Nora, Adam, and Grant.